The Bond That Breaks: Will Homosexuality Split the Church?

The Bond That Breaks: Will Homosexuality Split the Church?

by Don Williams

Box 259995
Los Angeles, CA 90025

TABLE of CONTENTS

PREFACE

A monumental crisis is upon the church. Avowed and practicing homosexual persons demand the sanction of their lifestyles and ordination into the professional clergy. I call this a crisis because it promises to disrupt congregations, shatter church structures, throw confusion into time-honored Biblical interpretation, change the social structure of our country, and revoke our fundamental view of Man as created by God as male and female.

Some people do not call this a crisis. Some call the homosexual challenge a blessing, a work of God. Here is our dilemma. Is this movement in the church a work of God or an error of man? We must not be too quick to answer. This is not merely a debate between those who believe in the Bible and those who don't. This is a question of how we understand the Bible. Some very sincere people want to redefine the traditional view of human sexuality, claiming that it is an incomplete understanding of God's plan. What is to be said of this?

We can only answer with a clear and thoughtful consideration of the whole issue. Careful scholarship and honest evaluation must mark our path as we seek the light of God's truth. This is our goal in this book. Our purpose is to hear all of the questions posed by the social sciences and modern theologians. Our plan is to reply to each fairly and honestly. Our goal is to seek the truth of God's Word.

We must be able not only to answer the question of homosexuality, but also to *respond* to it fully. We must know what we believe and why we believe it—both for the sake of the church and for the sake of the world. Finally, we trust God's presence with us as we engage in our study.

Don Williams
Los Angeles, California
1977

I. Introduction

Serving for eleven years on the staff of the Hollywood Presbyterian Church brought me into contact with many homosexual persons. Hollywood is a city of tarnished stars. The once proud palm-lined streets now show years of neglect and decay. The main boulevard hosts sleezy shops, bars, amusement arcades, tourist traps and porno movies. Hollywood also contains one of the major homosexual communities in the country.

While largely isolated from our church, some homosexual persons attended worship, others sought counseling, still others became Christians. When a generation hit the streets in the late 1960's Hollywood was a lure for many. We responded with a coffee house ministry—"The Salt Company"—and crash pads. As our community contacts escalated, so did our ministry to homosexual persons. Who were these people? How could we help them? What did Christ have to say to them and do with them? I had to answer these questions.

The two years which I have served on the National Task Force to Study Homosexuality for the United Presbyterian Church, USA, have exposed me to much of the literature of the homosexual advocates. The questions which are currently being raised by them are, to a large degree, the questions which I have addressed in this book. I trust that my dealing with them will aid you as you also seek to answer them responsibly.

The following episodes are offered to show that this study on homosexuality and the church is not merely academic. The crisis now facing us in the "homosexual question" is a crisis that has touched my life.

            o   o   o   o   o

The summons came in early evening while I was completing my work at Columbia University. Hailing a cab, I found my way through the traffic-clogged streets driving south from 116th and Broadway toward Park Avenue. Security rang the penthouse floor and in a moment I was face to face with one of the most powerful men in New York. The view was magnificent, the rooms were elegant— the setting was plush. But this was no night for pleasantries. My friend was clearly troubled and asked me to accompany him to the Americana Hotel where a suite was reserved.

We drove in strained silence. After the bellboy had led us to our accommodations and departed, my friend, without a word, reached in his trench coat and placed a loaded revolver on the coffee table. Now it came out in a torrent. **He was homosexual. He had had numberless young boys.** Someone had found out. Blackmail was in the offing. Suicide seemed to be the only alternative. What did I, as a Christian, have to say to him?

            o   o   o   o   o

The aging house we had rented stood in the Wilshire business district and was slated for destruction. Time had rotted its arrogant posture. It was, however, a perfect setting to take in scores of crashers whom we met on the streets of Hollywood needing a meal and a bed.

A former drag-queen came who had once reassigned soldiers he hated to the front lines in Viet Nam. A young heroin addict joined us with "homosexual tendencies." Many others came but the most perplexing and impressive was a giant hulk of a man in his late twenties. After his father had been sent to the penitentiary for murder, his home had been a series of juvenile institutions. Early homosexual experiences were common—yet there were heterosexual contacts as well.

Now, as an adult, he had a street wisdom that was disarming. He had heeded the call of Christ and was learning to live in his new found faith. The old destructive sexual urges, however, including violent rape, were still there, yet unacceptable to him because he knew that God wanted differently. This became the major conflict of his life. Contacts with the homosexual Metropolitan Community Church were shallow; he viewed it as little more than a gay bar. Yet the straight church was threatened by him and even tried excommunication as he sought spiritual help within it. A small support group of risking Christians stood with him, however, over several years of struggle.

One impressive night a birthday party was held in his honor. In attendance were a top official in Governor Reagan's administration, an outstanding dentist, and a lawyer. The close friend who had won him to Christ was also there, and several others. The evening concluded when this hulking man gathered us in a circle as he prayed a prayer of both gratefulness and suffering which left few eyes dry.

Slowly over the years his support group disintegrated as time took people away. Finally he returned to Ohio. Feeling desperate and alone, he died there of a heart attack.

o   o   o   o   o

I met him while he was in military uniform. He had just returned from Viet Nam. Loitering in the sanctuary after the service, his tears expressed his loneliness.

We ran into each other again years later. Now sporting fashion and flair, he drove his Porsche to a prestigious Bel Air church and looked every bit a part of the Hollywood scene. Over coffee he confessed his bisexuality. He had just broken up with a girl and had now swung over to the gay life. His father was a pastor—the fire-breathing kind. He left home in his teens after his dad had beaten him up, resolving that that was to be the last time. As he longed for his father's love the tears came freely to his eyes. "Do you hope to find that love in the gay bars?" I asked.

o   o   o   o   o

Speaking at a theological college in Canada on homosexuality and the church, I met an outstanding actor who was gay. Now out in the open, he was dealing with his homosexuality in the context of a Christ-centered fellowship. Love and trust were growing in a circle of friends. Earlier he had justified his reversions to the gay world because society told him he was sick. How then, he used to reason, could he be responsible for his actions? Turning to the gay church in Vancouver he found a false gospel of little more than social service. The message? Simply accept that you are gay and "adjust." Here he felt patronized. As he expressed it, "The kind father patted us boys on the head and told us that it's all right." For him this seemed to lack Biblical and personal depth.

Now in the evangelical community again, and having heard my lecture on homosexuality and the church, he expressed a new sense of freedom, "I know God loves me— without washing out the Biblical absolutes," he declared. He also felt a new honesty in relating to those around him; it was as if a door had been opened. What would the future hold? He sensed new confidence in answering that question.

o   o   o   o   o

He was a high official in a major Protestant denomination. He had served several churches before rising in the administrative ranks. We sat together during a conference when he asked if we could speak alone.

Privately, he confessed his double life. Although married, and with a family, he had fallen in love with a Roman Catholic priest who returned his affection. "Does your wife know?" I asked. He replied that she didn't. His failure to give her physical love was alibied to overwork. Perhaps not wanting to know the truth, she played his game. Why did he share this with me? I was from out of state—safely distant—and he had to tell someone.

¤   ¤   ¤   ¤   ¤

These personal encounters serve to underscore that this study is not written in the arid atmosphere of aloof scholarship and abstract theological debate. Nor is it written from a homophobic fear of gays. It is written from years of interaction with many homosexual persons. It also comes in the context of contemporary medical and psychological research on homosexuality, a serious commitment to the Bible as the Word of God and a deep and lasting concern for the church and those whom she serves. If the gospel is for all, it is also for gays. But the ability to reach gays with the truth of Christ comes only with an acute knowledge of their experience and a solid understanding of the faith and the hope it brings. Let us approach our study, then, with these aims before us: a thorough, comprehensive understanding which leads to truth, and a gracious, loving attitude which leads to new hope—the hope which we find in Christ.

II. Orientation and Background

Why is there such controversy and confusion today over the question of homosexuality? The answer comes from the collapse of two reigning orthodoxies: the Judeo-Christian tradition and Freudian psychology.

The first primary cause of discontent is the breakdown in the authority of the Bible and its historic interpretation. Until recently the general ethical norms in Western civilization have been nourished by a constant flow of Judeo-Christian teaching. A triumphant church set the standards of behavior for "Christian Europe" and the lands she colonized. Although secularization has undermined the institutional church since the Reformation, moral standards, imbedded deeply in the culture, have survived. If this is not true among most intellectuals, then it is at least true for the masses of people. The flower of accepted morality, however, cut from its roots in the Biblical tradition, soon withers, and we see that withering today.

At the same time, commonly held interpretations of the Bible are also under challenge from within the church itself. The assumption that the Scriptures clearly teach the sinfulness of homosexual practice is questioned now by many scholars. Theology is relativized as churches cannot agree among themselves as to what is true. Bishop Moore of the Episcopal church in New York ordained an avowed lesbian to the priesthood in 1976. Prior to that, William Johnson had been the first avowed homosexual person to be ordained into the United Church of Christ. Thus the question of homosexuality is held to be open by many sincere, inquiring Christians. If the theologians are in confusion among themselves as to what the Bible says or means, and if denominations are beginning to ordain avowed homosexual persons, why should lay people continue to hold traditional positions that are more and more debated, out-moded or simply wrong? This is the dilemma that many are facing.

The second primary cause for confusion is the breakdown in the traditional authority of Freudian psychology in the secular culture. For Freud, homosexuality was an illness. It resulted from an improper relationship between the growing child and his or her family. Since Freud held sexual identity and behavior to be learned from the parents, homosexuality is an arresting of the normal growth to heterosexuality which takes place through a healthy family. For example, Freud sums up childhood development for the male as follows: first, a concentration on his mother and an identification with his father as the image of what he is to become. Next, intense sexual wishes toward his mother with a desire to replace his father (Oedipus complex, named after the king who unknowingly killed his father and married his mother). Later this dissolves when the child normally identifies with his father rather than his mother. Freud concludes, "In this way the passing of the Oedipus complex would consolidate the masculinity in the boy's character. . . ." [1]

Freud admitted, however, that since children are originally bisexual, not all make this step. For it to happen, the boy's masculine sexual disposition must be stronger than his feminine sexual disposition.[2] Freud held, "A boy has not merely an ambivalent attitude towards his father and an affectionate object-relation towards his mother, but at the same time he also behaves like a girl and displays an affectionate feminine attitude to his father and a corresponding hostility and jealousy towards his mother." [3] This bisexuality was the complicating factor in understanding the child's earliest identification with his parents. It even led Freud to propose that the child's ambivalence towards them was due to a biological bisexuality and not a consequence of his psychological development. [4] Nevertheless, the Freudian position was traditionally established in the Oedipus complex where the male child grows to maturity through identification with his father whom he "replaces" as he then projects his love for his mother upon other women. In this way he becomes a male heterosexual. Any deviation from this means stunted growth or "sickness." For the secular mind, homosexuality is no longer a "sin," but a deviation from the norm of heterosexuality and the traditions of almost two thousand years of western sexual ethics. Although Freud had reduced man to a complex organization of biological drives and denied his spiritual nature, secularized people could still view homosexuality as abhorrent.

Nevertheless, as we have already asserted, both of these historic views are under severe challenge today. What then are the sources of this challenge? What has given it popular footing? There are several answers. The first is the impact of the Kinsey report on human sexuality. The second is the surfacing of liberation movements with their demands for full civil rights. The third is the youth-inspired counter-culture which arose in opposition to the "technological society" and the Viet Nam war, and the fourth is the critique of classical psychoanalytical assumptions and methods by other social scientists. Let us examine each of these contributions to the homosexual challenge.

Alfred Kinsey's research into human sexual behavior was revolutionary for our present understanding of homosexuality. To begin with, Kinsey's statistics were devastating. He wrote, " . . . the data will show there is only about half of the male population whose sexual behavior is exclusively heterosexual, and there are only a few percent who are exclusively homosexual." [5] Thus there are millions upon millions of men in the United States who have had homosexual feelings or experiences. According to Kinsey, fifteen to fifty percent of all males are capable of responding to homosexual stimulation. One out of three have had an actual homosexual experience, and they are as likely to have that experience in their twenties, thirties, or forties as in adolescence. [6] Thus for Kinsey, "The heterosexuality or homosexuality of many individuals is not an all-or-none proposition. . . . The record . . . shows that there is a considerable portion of the population whose members have combined, within their individual histories, both homosexual and heterosexual experience and/or psychic responses." [7] Furthermore, twenty five percent of all adult white males have had or will have some distinct and continuing homosexual experience. One in ten is more or less exclusively homosexual for three years or more between the ages of sixteen and fifty five. [8] Humphrey's comment on Kinsey's work is apt: "The sense of utter isolation was lifted from the gay population." [9]

Not only was the incidence of homosexuality now seen to be widespread, it was also a matter of degree and not kind. Moreover, unorthodox sexual practices were also discovered by Kinsey to be characteristic of heterosexual persons as well as homosexual persons. No longer could homosexual persons be stigmatized as acting "unnaturally." [10] Thus Kinsey's study emphasized that homosexuality was but one part of the continuum of human sexual behavior.

While Kinsey's research has been challenged by Edmund Bergler because of selective statistics, neurotic volunteers, and the unjustifiable inclusion of early child-hood same-sex experiences in proving that homosexuality is widespread,[11] C. A. Tripp notes Kinsey's vindication by the American Statistical Association as having produced "the highest quality of work ever done in the field." [12] Regardless of the scientific accuracy of Kinsey's findings, the general public was now faced with the question. Can so many millions of people be "unnatural" in their sexual preference or dislocated in their proper sexual develop-ment to heterosexuality?

While Kinsey created a climate for the re-evaluation of homosexuality, especially in the academic community, it took the civil rights movement to bring gay people "out of the closet." Sociologist Laud Humphreys writes, "Two preconditions of a social movement are the oppressive sense of intolerable reality and the vision of conceivable change." [13] The moral and social preconditions for the gay liberation movement were the Black and Women's movements which presented similar challenges to the traditional social structure.[14] They combined both the "sense of intolerable reality" in the present and the dis-tinct possibility of change. Thus Humphreys concludes, "Like the student protest that flowered in the late 1960's, gay liberation had its roots in the older civil rights movements, with a history stretching back into the 1950's." [15] The gay movement copied both the civil rights leaders' rhetoric and strategies.[16] Similar to the Black movement, the early stages developed leadership from ministers and lawyers. The Rev. Troy Perry, founder of the Metropolitan Community Church, emerged as the "Martin Luther Queen" of the cause.[17] This was followed by the re-evaluation of homosexuality by the social scientists. As a liberation movement gay activists sought to end police harrassment and to gain full civil rights. In order to achieve this gays needed greater cohesion. This was supplied by the youth counter-culture.

Humphreys notes that older homosexuals had lived in a scared, exploited and exploitative community. With the arrival of the youth counter-culture, however, a new, positive identity emerged. For Humphreys the "development of this counter-culture on America's streets and campuses was an essential condition for the gay revolution. It supplied special skills, an ideology and the necessary reinforcement to increase autonomy for the youthful gays." [18] In its early stages it often embraced the politics of the radical new left. Now, however, it has matured from confrontation to subversion,[19] and by 1972 little remained of radical gay liberation.[20]

Nevertheless, gay leaders are now calling for a separate gay culture as a preliminary step before integration with "straight" society. Gay psychologist Don Clark writes, "As the Blacks learned before us, integration is not possible until you cease to conform to stereotype and recognize your strength and the goodness of your identity." [21] Thus he calls for gay ceremonies similar to heterosexual weddings and funerals. He continues, "We need to develop our own psychology, sociology, and anthropology—our study of ourselves and our culture—and then present it proudly to the rest of the world so that they can join us in celebration. We are Gay. We are growing. And we are learning how to be glad." [22]

In the wake of Kinsey's study, the gay liberation movements, and a new developing gay culture, there has emerged a re-evaluation of research presuppositions and methodology in the academic community. Perhaps the major target of attack in this re-evaluation has been traditional Freudian psychoanalysis. For example, Tripp is critical of the Freudian school's overemphasis on parental roles in a child's identity formation. He suggests that since most of the early analysts were Jewish, and the family is essential for Jewish identity, this became the focus. Kinsey, however, has shown that it is the peer group more than the family which influences a child's identity and values.[23] For Tripp, Freud's "primal family determinism" is a scientific curiosity which offered facile systematic explanations and deductive conclusions.[24]

Furthermore, the Freudian understanding of homosexuality, was doomed at the beginning, for Tripp, because it presupposed its origin in damaged or blocked heterosexuality. This focus on the negative causes was pointless because all sexual attractions are based on positive motives, " . . . the real or imagined benefits a person hopes to gain by a sexual conquest or by 'possessing' the partner."[25] Thus homosexuality must be studied in terms of its own motivations in order to understand the various needs being met by persons seeking same-sex relationships. Calling off the neurotic hunt for childhood damage by the Freudians, Tripp concludes that homosexuality has proved ". . . the utter embarrassment of every formal psychiatric theory without exception."[26]

George Weinberg also critiques the methodology of psychoanalysts. Too often they have based their views of homosexuality as sickness upon the limited sample of troubled people seeking their help.[27] The methods of change employed by behavioral scientists in the 1960's have also been discounted. Weinberg judges that these aversive techniques ". . . range from the zany to the gruesome. Two of them—brain surgery and emetic persuasion [for example, induced vomiting]—make unpleasant reading."[28] In such reconditioning of homosexual persons behavioral psychologists were "sniping at a human relationship, as rich and full as their own love relationships. . . ."[29] This makes as much sense for Weinberg as shooting a popgun at a battleship.

Sociologists Martin Weinberg and Colin Williams, following Kinsey, criticize psychoanalysts for assuming that people are either heterosexual or homosexual rather than viewing human sexuality on a continuum.[30] They also fault psychiatrists and psychologists in their methodological failure to do cross-cultural comparisons.[31]

Weinberg and Williams then offer a new approach in the study of homosexuality which proposes that it be viewed as a natural variant of human sexual expression. If homosexuality is not a sickness, there is no reason to search for causes or cures. Moreover, heterosexuality is not the norm for human sexuality other " . . . than in a statistical sense."[32]

Now rather than viewing homosexuality as a condition, attention is focused on how the homosexual person is affected by his social situation.[33] What makes homosexuality "deviant," therefore, is not psychological make-up but "the fact that people differentiate, stigmatize and penalize alleged homosexuals."[34] Deviance lies in society, and it is society which must be changed—not the homosexual person. Here we see sociological preparation for the demand that the church (along with the rest of society) must cease its "deviant" behavior toward homosexual persons.

No wonder that with the current critique of presuppositions and techniques, the formal associations of psychiatrists and psychologists have reconsidered and reversed their positions on homosexuality. Near the end of 1973 the American Psychiatric Association omitted homosexuality from its diagnostic list of emotional disorders[35] and in 1975 the American Psychological Association urged "all mental health professionals to take the lead in removing the stigma of mental illness that has long been associated with homosexual orientation."[36]

It is into this crucible of claim and counter-claim that

the church is thrown. As we conclude this brief orientation several questions arise which demand answers: How should we define homosexuality? What does the Bible teach? What then is theologically normative for the church? What are the origins and goals of homosexuality? How does our theology relate to modern research into human sexuality? Are homosexual persons sinful? Are they sick? Are they deviant, or are society and the church deviant? Can homosexual persons be changed? If they can, should they? What about membership and leadership in the church for practicing and advocating homosexual persons? How should the church deal with the gay community?

Before rushing to answer these questions, we must investigate the viable positions held today with regard to homosexuality. To champion only a Freudian stance or to rule out all psychoanalytic work *a priori* is both premature and reactive. To ignore the inquiries of modern sex research would also be a mistake. Let us therefore turn to summarize some of the modern researchers.

III. Contemporary Views
of Homosexuality

Current scholarly research on the origin and meaning of homosexuality is both intense and diverse. Our first area of interest is definitions: Who is a homosexual person? Next the causes of homosexuality will concern us. Then we will ask the difficult question of whether homosexual persons should seek change. Also we will give some attention to the problem of homophobia.

Four positions, reflecting several fields of scientific research and embracing widely differing view points, will be reviewed. We will begin with the more "classical" representative of psychoanalysis in Lawrence Hatterer and turn then to the sex research of C. A. Tripp. This will be followed by George Weinberg's analysis of homophobia and then the gay advocacy of Don Clark. After summarizing each author we will offer a brief critique, reserving full comments for our final conclusion.

The purpose of surveying these four men is to listen to the questions which the gay world is posing and to hear their answers before we turn to the Scriptures.

Lawrence Hatterer

Hatterer writes *Changing Homosexuality in the Male* out of extensive clinical research, the sustained counseling of over 200 homosexual males from 1953-1970, and a command of the literature in the field. Who is a homosexual person? Hatterer begins by surveying the answers.

As a biologist, Kinsey views human sexuality on a continuum and therefore refuses to establish clear, neat categories. He writes, "It would encourage clearer thinking . . . if persons were not characterized as heterosexual or homosexual, but as individuals who have had certain amounts of heterosexual experience and certain amounts of homosexual experience." [1]

After surveying homosexuality in seventy-six societies, anthropologists Clellan Ford and Frank Beach conclude that in some cultures 100 percent of the males engage in both homosexual and heterosexual activity. Since many men and women in our own society are equally capable of the same activity (as is also true of many species of subhuman primates), homosexual or heterosexual tendencies are not mutually exclusive or even opposed to each other. [2]

Sociologist Evelyn Hooker studied male homosexual persons outside of clinical settings. She concludes that homosexuality is a "many-faceted phenomenon" in both the individual's experience, in society, and in its determination by psychodynamic, biological, cultural and situational variables. [3] What is important for Hooker is not if one is a homosexual, but what kind of a homosexual one is, and here we meet endless variety.

Samuel Hadden offers a psychoanalytic perspective. He views homosexuality as a symptom of an underlying personality disorder, or "defective personality organization." [4] Similarly, Judd Marmor defines the clinical homosexual person as an adult motivated by "a definite preferential erotic attraction to members of the same sex and who usually (but not necessarily) engages in overt sexual relations with them." [5] Such a definition is not merely quantitative, as in Kinsey, but is also qualitative in nature.[6]For Marmor, homosexual adaptation occurs when there is a combination of impaired gender identity, a fear of close contact with the opposite sex, and opportunity for same-sex experiences.[7]

After surveying these different views, Hatterer himself isolates one common denominator: the experience by the male of active or passive sexual arousal by another male in dream, fantasy, impulse, or action.[8] Each definition of homosexuality contains some truth and the different disciplines then lead Hatterer to his thesis: the causes of homosexuality are multi-determined and require "multidimensional treatment." [9] While Hatterer clearly sees heterosexuality as the norm for human sexuality, all homosexual persons cannot be changed. Avoiding simplistic answers Hatterer sums up his experience, "I learned who could be helped and began to systematize the insights and therapeutic techniques that could produce newly fulfilled lives, free from the compulsions, fears, depressions, and self-destructive impulses that plague such men. I also learned how to help those committed to their homosexual practices or to a homosexual way of life to cope with their lives without prejudice or hopelessness." [10]

Since the origins of homosexuality are multi-faceted,[11] Hatterer accepts the major perspectives on etiology which have dominated research over the years.[12] He offers numerous combinations of factors, of which only a sample is summarized here.

The first perspectives on origins come from the family. The homosexual person may have a strong fixation toward his mother along with the inability to leave her. This causes overidentification with her and her feminine, passive role. There may also be a negative effect on the homosexual person's relationship to women because of his mother's "dominant, binding, seductive, overprotective, passive-aggressive controlling or possessive behavior." [13]

In the case of the father there may be one or a combination of "absence, indifference, emasculation, aggressiveness, excessive dominance, hostility, rejection, partial and/or total inability to identify with his son." [14]

Then also the homosexual person must relate to himself. He may have castration fears or excessive self-love due to the absence of any male figure with which to identify. He may also be compensating for the lack of male identity by the erotic possession of an idealized male figure. [15]

Male homosexuality may also come from an inadequate relationship between the mother and the father. The classical view is that a homosexual person is formed by ". . . a dominant, agressive, hostile, binding, but hypercritical mother . . . combined with a passive, ineffectual, rejecting, indifferent father." [16] Hatterer also suggests that there may be other contributing factors from brothers and sisters and close relatives.

Beyond the family is the surrounding culture. [17] There a sustained exposure to homosexual persons while erotic identity is being formed may result in homosexuality. Also a strong exposure to sexual stimuli with heterosexual prohibitions may leave only homosexual alternatives. [18]

Hatterer next turns to interpersonal relationships. A child may be emasculated by male peers, reject all competitive and aggressive social group activities, or establish possessive contacts with male ideals due to a need for "maleness" or due to the lack of emotional contact with his father. [19]

In light of this extensive catalogue, Hatterer concludes that it is now plain why no single cause-and-effect theory can explain the origins of homosexuality. [20] He also cautions that it has not been established which factors are more important than others in forming the homosexual person.[21] While most psychiatrists still find the roots of homosexuality in the family, there are hundreds of other variables from the person himself and his environment.[22] Homosexuality is, to be sure, learned behavior. Psychiatrists are coming to agree "that homosexuals are not born but made and that genetic, hereditary, constitutional, glandular, or hormonal factors have no significance in causing homosexuality." [23]

What then should the therapeutic response of the psychatrist be? For Hatterer the first step is to abandon all preconceptions about the causes of homosexuality. Then the doctor must listen to his patients with a completely open mind and begin to recognize significant clues.[24]

How then can male homosexual persons be changed? To begin with they must want to change. The patient's ability to collaborate with the therapist and the depth of the need to change will largely determine the outcome of therapy.[25] The motivation for change will come by an emotional and intellectual alienation from one's homosexual identity. Then too, the younger the patient the better. Also, he is more treatable if he has had few overt homosexual experiences or if he has not yet "come out" and identified himself with the homosexual community.[26] If, however, the patient reports no heterosexual attraction, impulse, or arousal, he is untreatable.[27]

The role of the therapist is to provide hope for change to the one who is homosexual. He must avoid simply focusing on the sexual issue, a "hypersexual approach," and treat the total person. He also must continually support the patient's attitudes of alienation from his homosexuality, reinforce his male identity and support his efforts toward female contact.[28]

For the remainder of his study, Hatterer offers clinical methods for change illustrated by extensive case histories.

What are his results? Of one hundred forty-four men who have been treated and followed up, "forty-nine patients recovered, nineteen patients partially recovered, seventy-six remained homosexual." [29] As Hatterer remarks to a changing homosexual male who is afraid of marriage because it would ruin his potential wife, "All I can tell you is that I've treated many men who were homosexuals who became heterosexual and didn't return to their homosexuality and didn't ruin their wives' lives . . . It's relative and each case has to be seen in its own context . . . and with its dozens of variables." [30] What then can we say about Hatterer?

"Cause," "treatment," "cure," "change." These are all words which Hatterer uses in his discussion of homosexuality. They reveal to us his basic view of human sexuality. Heterosexuality is the norm and homosexuality is a deviation from that norm and is not healthy behavior. Therefore the homosexual person should be aided to move into a heterosexual orientation. Hatterer also proposes that homosexuality is learned behavior that has no significant relationship to genetic, hereditary, glandular, or hormonal factors. As we shall see, this is a very significant distinction.

But, while Hatterer accepts heterosexuality as the norm, he offers no real ground for this. Concluding that homosexuality is learned makes Hatterer optimistic that it can be unlearned for many people. But again, apart from easier living in a predominately heterosexual culture, why would one opt for the time and expense of therapy, especially in light of today's gay liberation movement which insists that gay is good?

Hatterer desires to make people whole, but wholeness apart from a new spiritual life will only be defined in psychological or sociological dimensions. This is clearly inadequate. Thus in the areas of both motivation and goals, "why?" and "to what end?" Hatterer is unsatisfactory. To the homosexual who comes to Christ there is great hope for change. The hope for change is found in Christ, the need for change is established in God's revealed order of man as male and female.

We turn now to a contrasting viewpoint in the context of contemporary social science disciplines and cross-cultural sexual research.

C. A. Tripp

In *The Homosexual Matrix*, Tripp deals with both heterosexuality and homosexuality. Quickly disassociating himself from traditional psychiatric viewpoints, he writes, "Perhaps the single most troublesome assumption has been that every mature person would be heterosexual were it not for various fears and neuroses developed from parental and social misfortunes." [31] How then should homosexuality be viewed? Tripp responds that biology deserves the first word in understanding sexuality in general and homosexuality in particular. [32] Why is this so? Because for Tripp, nature is all we have. Society views masturbation, anal intercourse, and homosexuality as abnormal and against nature, "as if there were some source other than nature from which they could have come." [33] Following Kinsey, Tripp views human sexuality on a continuum where all variations are natural and the traditional categories of heterosexual/homosexual must be rejected. Thus, for Tripp, it is tempting to conclude that there is a homosexual potential in everyone quite ready to be activated. [34] Even monogamy is "patently moralistic or . . . simply naive," and sophisticated observers reject all such criteria. [35]

In observing the evolutionary development of mammals, we see that the control of sex has moved from glands and reflexes ("instincts") to "the heights of cortical management" and a huge diversity of sexual expression has resulted.[36] While sex for lower mammals has specific "physiologic controls" which are activated by cues directly related to reproduction,[37] in human beings it is the cerebral cortex, containing ninety percent of the brain mass, which has taken over sexual behavior as a learning task.[38]

For this reason, when homosexual males were treated with sex hormones (testosterone) on the assumption that their deficiency caused homosexuality, they became more like themselves; their homosexual sex drives increased without any directional change.[39] Thus for Tripp, "Human sexuality is exceedingly variable, deriving its directionality (especially its final targeting) from what is individually learned and experienced in personal and social settings."[40] As the individual develops a sexual value system and discards weaker alternatives, certain partners and patterns become the "salient imperatives of his highest sexual response."[41]

Why then are most people heterosexual? Because, responds Tripp, their upbringing has geared them to want to be.[42] Family life serves as a model for what they are to become and receives its support from the religious and social tradition. Furthermore, sexual attraction thrives, not just on easy sexual contact, but on a degree of tension and distance especially realized by male and female partners.[43] Tripp adds that a considerable amount of evidence shows that both sexes have always affirmed the primacy of men and the subservience of women, in order to maintain sexual attraction by tension and difference.[44] While partners need complementation in the sexual polarities, too much blending dissolves their sexual relationship, thus the need to be close and the spark of sexual attraction are at cross-purposes.[45]

In summary, heterosexuality is learned. Tripp asserts, "A specific heterosexual motivation can start with social suggestions which lead to real or imagined sex experiences, events which then simply condition men and women to respond to each other." [46]

What then are the origins of homosexuality? For Tripp, certainly not any particular family structure. What really matters is the conceptual framework in which sex is cast. But here there is a dazzling array of possibilities and it is difficult to know what goes with what. [47] Let's look at some of the variables.

In societies where homosexuality is lauded or approved it will be more prevalent. [48] More than this, however, Tripp sees much evidence to suggest that the way a society views maleness and the values given to it will control the amount of homosexuality. [49] In societies, such as among some Indians, where males are non-competitive and more cooperative, homosexuality is low. Where there are male concepts of the winner and the hero, however, homosexuality is readily activated. [50] Among Hindus, where there is little tradition for individual male development and little admiration for same-sex attributes, there is little homosexuality. Graeco-Roman male ideals are in sharp contrast to this and produce a corresponding rise in homosexuality. [51]

Why does the male ideal produce homosexuality? Tripp answers that young boys who have identity problems, seeing a sharp contrast between themselves and the culture's male ideal, tend to eroticize that ideal, and then seek to possess it sexually. Thus, they would import more masculinity into themselves. A boy set apart from his peer group envies the other boys. This can easily lead him to an erotic solution. At the same time, a boy near the male ideal may find his aspirations soar ahead of his achievements and likewise find a similar erotic solution.[52] Both types of boys may become homosexual.

Moreover, a young boy may easily associate his awakening sexuality with maleness before any consciousness of heterosexual possibilities. This is especially true of boys reaching early puberty. They may make a crucial association between their own genitalia and sexual identity. This is then easily extended to other male attributes.[53] Eroticizing objects gives them greater value. Tripp notes, "Even the confident and utterly secure male who has eroticized male attributes is ready to improve what he has by sexually importing refinements and additions from an admired partner."[54] Such homosexuality has "value based origins."

A further cause is, of course, an initial sexual encounter with another homosexual person. For this experience to have lasting significance, however, there must be a variety of conditions including a pre-established sexual value system, sexual tension in the encounter, and emotional impact.[55] For Tripp, values more often lead to experience than experience to values.[56] Thus the simple seduction of a child is powerless to start a sexual pattern.

Tripp concludes that there is no single original influence which alone will be definitive in homosexuality. One's final sexual orientation depends upon how the various parts of that orientation have reinforced each other in producing a structure, value system and pattern of responses. The directionality of a person toward homosexuality will depend upon how effectively he purifies his aims, and rejects competing alternatives.[57] Thus the homosexual person develops an aversion to the female as he eroticizes the male and all gender related items.

What then is the goal for a homosexual relationship? Tripp responds, "The symbolic possession of those attributes of a partner which, when added to one's own, fill out the illusion of completeness."[58]

The homosexual need to import masculinity has immediate bearing for Tripp on two related questions: male homosexual promiscuity and ongoing homosexual relationships.

Tripp notes that promiscuity always implies a desire for something more than can be obtained from a single partner.[59] It was Kinsey who first found out that many homosexual men have hundreds, or even thousands of relationships before middle age. This is seldom matched by the most active heterosexual person.[60] Also this promiscuity is relatively prevalent.[61] Why so? There are several reasons including the high male sex-drive, his easy, fast sexual response, the species-history of the sexual chase, male visual orientation, and the driving power of fantasy.[62] In our culture, moreover, males are "immersed in a pool of arousing sexual stimuli. . . . "[63] Then, too, there is the social reinforcement of status by "playing the field" and married homosexual men can avoid commitments by anonymous sex.[64] Furthermore, there are the ego-rewards of conquest (or being conquered), and the affirmation of one's market value.[65]

Tripp concludes that males have a vast capacity to respond to new partners. This is activated by reading value connotations into the bodily features of the kinds of partners they have previously eroticized.[66] Male sexual promiscuity, unknown among lesbians, comes from circumstantial opportunity combined with the "escalating effect of males dealing with males."[67]

What about ongoing male homosexual relationships? Tripp suggests that while such relationships seem to be rare, it may be because they are less visible. Nevertheless, it is true that for the male: 1) he is highly promiscuous, 2) most of his relationships do not last, 3) he can and does maintain a substantial number of ongoing relationships.[68] These ongoing relationships usually have a limited time span in sexual interest of five to seven years. Many lesbian couples give up overt sexual relationships within two to three years.[69] While healthy heterosexual relationships are rich in tension and stimulating contrasts, homosexual relationships "are overclose, fatigueprone, and are often adjusted to such narrow, trigger sensitive tolerances. . . . "[70]

What then about the attempt to change the orientation of homosexual persons? This comes largely from psychiatrists who are the guardians of society, committed to present heterosexual norms.[71] Thus, they value the attempt to change homosexual persons whom they often see during a crisis of self-doubt. The fact is, however, that for Tripp, homosexuality and psychotherapy have been bad for each other.[72] Homosexuality "has damaged psychotherapy almost beyond its capacity to recover." [73] Thus the whole field has been quietly repudiated by scientists.[74] Why is this? Because validated changes in people who are homosexual "are nowhere to be found." [75] Tripp continues, "[There is no change] for the simple and not so simple reason that the adult human being's sexual response rests at bottom on a massive, cortically organized, sexual value system which is impervious to the trivial intrusions launched against it by what amount to social concerns (concerns which can muster their support from no more than a fragment of frontal lobe authority)." [76]

What then is the real trouble with homosexuality? Tripp answers that homosexual persons threaten a conformist society and are personally vulnerable because of it.[77] Their diversity offers us richness, however, but at the expense of our social traditions.[78]

How shall we evaluate Tripp? To begin with, he offers a multitude of valid insights into both heterosexuality and homosexuality. Like Hatterer, Tripp sees our sexual preference as learned, going beyond simple animal instinct. For Tripp, however, our freedom is an evolutionary accomplishment rather than the gift of God. For him, nature is all we have. No wonder he views monogamy as naive and promiscuity as natural. Here is an abandonment of all morality based on absolute values. Tripp unfortunately fails to see that as human beings we must ask, "Is it right?" We have a conscience because we participate in a moral order created by God. To deny this is naive.

A useful insight is Tripp's view of society's role in creating homosexuality through heroic ideals and resulting erotic solutions. In so far as this is true, it provides a commentary upon the fallenness of the social order.

Tripp is blind to the potential for change in our sexual preference. He speaks of "trivial intrusions" upon our massive sexual value system by "social concerns." While some may be victims of these, the entrance of Christ into one's life is no trivial intrusion. Furthermore, God's call for us to live according to His divine order and will is no mere "social concern." Tripp's own values and assumptions depreciate the potential for the gospel to alter radically human life and experience. As we have said, what can be learned can potentially be unlearned. What is necessary at that point is a sense of absolute values to guide our choices. If nature is all we have, as Tripp supposes, then we live in darkness. God's intrusive revelation of Himself in Scripture can be our only light.

We turn now to another perspective on homosexuality which confronts a basic cultural sickness: homophobia.

George Weinberg

The term "homophobia" was first coined by Weinberg in *Society and the Healthy Homosexual.* As his title suggests, it is society, not the homosexual person, that is "perverted," as it demands conformity and irrationally fears people who are homosexual. For Weinberg, the key issue is not whether one is a homosexual but how one handles his homosexuality.[79] Thus the focus is shifted from the nature of homosexuality, to how one acts out a homosexual life-style in the context of society.

Weinberg begins his discussion not with the origins of homosexuality, but with the origins of homophobia. This is, in part, because his program is to change the way society deals with homosexual persons and in part because he asserts that we cannot know why some people are homosexual. He writes, "The fact is that the combination of physiological readiness and social experience resulting in the development of *any* erotic preference—homosexual or heterosexual—is so intricate that science has not been able to fathom it as yet." [80] It is possible that parents have nothing to do with the origins of homosexuality. Perhaps pleasurable homosexual experiences when mental processes are receptive motivate a desire for more of the same. In any case, for Weinberg, homosexuality comes from several interrelated coincidences.[81]

While Weinberg is in doubt about the origins of homosexuality, he is not in doubt over the origins of homophobia. Its chief motives lie in the Christian religious ideals of monogamy and sex for procreation; the secret fear among many of being homosexual themselves; repressed envy toward homosexual persons who do not have to fulfill society's sexual stereotypes; the apparent threat to society's values by nonconformists; and the absence in homosexual persons of the magical device for coping with the fear of death by finding a vicarious immortality in their children.[82]

For Weinberg, traditional psychoanalysis has reinforced homophobia by viewing homosexual persons as sick and by seeking to change them by aligning them to society's heterosexual norm. Weinberg asserts, however, that calling homosexual persons psychologically sick is meaning-less.[83] The Freudian assumption that homosexuality comes from some failure to reach heterosexuality is both irrelevant and false since we must concern ourselves with our future, not with our past. The homosexual person's future is not to be changed since heterosexuality is not the goal for human sexuality. In critique of Hatterer's psychotherapeutic attempts to reorient people who are homosexual, Weinberg writes, "In place of the Hell used by preachers to frighten homosexuals, psychoanalysis warns' homosexuals that they will suffer a dissolute life, an incomplete existence, an old age spent in misery." [84]

Why then should homosexual persons not be changed? Not only, answers Weinberg, because the heterosexual ideal is invalid, but also because, functionally, they cannot be changed. Every method of change employed is severely doubted by most practitioners.[85] The truth is that people who are homosexual have no reasonable chance for change and therefore they will probably suffer more, not less, as a result of treatment.[86]

What then should society's concern be? Weinberg's answer is the creation of healthy homosexual persons. The following definition of homosexuality is ventured by Weinberg: "To be homosexual is to have an erotic preference for members of one's own sex. One may be homosexual for a minute, an hour, a day, or a lifetime." [87] Thus, by this definition, homosexuality may be the experience of most, and it is highly elastic.

What society has done is to create homophobia by telling children that the goal of life is monogamous, heterosexual marriage replete with children.[88] In relation to this, children are then socialized to be revolted by homosexual feelings and actions.

The attitude of homophobia is made to seem right when people act upon it. Weinberg writes, "Once a person acts

on any belief—in this case, disdain for homosexuals—
among the outcomes is that he makes the belief seem
righter than ever." [89] Actions hold attitudes in place,
and fear of homosexual feelings is learned by the fear
of ridicule or ostracism. The neurotic solution then, is a
flight into guilt.[90] Thus the homosexual person interna-
lizes the culture's homophobia.

How then can healthy homosexual persons be created?
The only way to change the negative attitude toward homosexuality is by disallowing it throughout the whole range
of one's behaviour,[91] because no attitude can survive
without a corresponding action.[92] Thus the homosexual
person must identify all action springing from guilt over
homosexuality and eliminate it in order to become healthy.
By so doing, not only will the symptom be changed, the
underlying attitude will also go with it.[93] As a homosexual person acts in accordance with his or her belief, that
belief becomes a conviction.[94] Thus, if a homosexual
person is to be free from homophobia, there must be the
conviction that it is wrong and an honest motive to eliminate it.[95]

In conclusion then, why for Weinberg should one who
is homosexual not seek to become heterosexual? Because
the attempt to change will be certain to fail; it makes one
feel that he or she is one of nature's misfortunes; it in-
tensifies society's clinging to conventionality; it enlarges
fear, guilt, and regret; it stultifies sexual fantasy; and
it is an assault on the right of people to do as they please
as long as no one else is harmed.[96] For Weinberg, it
is society that is sick and society that must be changed.
The "homosexual problem" is the problem of condemning
variety in human existence." [97]

In evaluating Weinberg we admit that he puts his finger
upon a key issue which must not be dodged. Homophobia
is a problem in our culture. Too often the church has

rejected rather than redeemed homosexual persons. We easily believe in the power of sin rather than in the power of Christ. Thus homosexual persons are unwelcome by us and Christians who are homosexual live hidden lives.

At the same time, Weinberg wants a society of variety without moral judgment. He fails to see that the Biblical standards of monogamy and heterosexual relationships need not produce homophobia. Sin must be exposed and at the same time, the sinner must be loved, forgiven and accepted. If the gospel is a call to sinners it means they're welcome by God. To abandon monogamy, however, does not mean "variety," it means anarchy. The God who welcomes us calls us to a new life in His will.

Weinberg opposes the attempt to change homosexual persons because for him they cannot be changed. At the same time, he asserts that no attitude can survive without a corresponding action. If this is true, a change in homosexual action could change a homosexual attitude. The case is not as closed as Weinberg supposes.

While opposing the immorality of homophobia, we must also oppose the immorality of sexual chaos and the abandonment of God's order. Our true humanity is at stake here.

Finally, we turn now to the position of full gay advocacy by Don Clark, who is himself homosexual.

Don Clark

In *Loving Someone Gay*, Clark defines a homosexual, or in his preferred title a "gay" person, as follows: "I am willing to consider the man Gay if he is aware of sexual, emotional, spiritual and intellectual attraction to some other men and knows himself to be capable of acting behaviorally on that attraction." [98] For Clark this is no liability. Rather than meaning that a gay person is unable to have a satisfying heterosexual relationship, it means that he or she is able to have a satisfying homosexual relationship.[99] At the same time, Clark refuses to make his definition static. To be gay is to be capable of loving someone of the same gender, but a gay person can still love someone of the other gender, too.[100] Thus for Clark, gay can mean exclusive love for the same sex or inclusive love for both sexes. He asserts, "If you are emotionally, intellectually and bodily attracted to people of the same gender, you know it. You may be far from wanting to admit it, but you are Gay." [101] This is true even if you have a similar sexual attraction to the opposite sex.

What then is the origin of same-sex attraction? For Clark it begins at birth. In infancy we simply seek pleasant sensations wherever they come from. As we grow up we are taught that some feelings are bad and that we are not to express them in behavior.[102] Thus Clark concludes that "in a sense, we are all born Gay, capable of moving toward pleasant homosexual sensations. It is a gift given to each human at birth, but because it is discouraged in our part of the world, only some of us keep the gift." [103]

It is society that socializes out our homosexual feelings. They lie below the surface, however, ready to re-emerge in contrast to our sexist training. Clark continues, "The secret shame of these hidden feelings is the dragon at the gateway of full self-awareness." [104] Thus full self-awareness will come when all recognize that they are gay—that is, capable of loving the same sex and able to act out on that love. It is the gay person who is "normal," the most in touch, the new cultural ideal.

In developing the new ideal, Clark attacks the polar opposites and dualities of society.[105] A person attracted to his or her sexual opposite is only half a person.[106] The really strong person is androgynous, or attracted to one like himself. For Clark, as a gay person is reprogrammed to become self-respecting, he or she will be increasingly attracted to others who are similar and as loveable as one's newly evolved self.[107] Thus the gay person is more whole, having rejected the male-female polarities, and having recovered the gay reality of infancy. As Clark puts it, "While most of the rest of the population struggles with the *half-lives assigned to them* . . . we can be whole as humans." [108]

Having based homosexuality in infancy, Clark is disinterested in why some people grow up gay. All of the reasons lie in cultural conditioning. For Clark, the search for the causes of homosexuality makes as little sense as the search for the causes of heterosexuality, namely, why some people follow the culture and tune out their same-sex feelings.[109] The only reason to find "causes" is to alter the homosexual condition. This, however, by Clark's analysis, is like trying to alter human nature itself, it is doomed to fail. The attempts to explain homosexual origins come from the anti-gay myths of our culture.[110] We simply do not know why some people retain their awareness of attraction to the same sex and other people lose that awareness.[111]

What then must happen to liberate gay people (all of us?)? First, the hostile environment must be changed.[112] In a homophobic world, as Clark writes, "You are usually cautioned to mend your ways, repent, get well, confess, pray for forgiveness, or at least keep silent." [113] But all of this leads to failure and rage too often turned inward in suicide. The homophobic person, according to Clark, is fighting unacceptable feelings inside himself or herself which are probably homosexual.[114] Thus, psychotherapy should be turned on the homophobic.[115] The end of homophobia will mean that gay people can live without any more particular difficulty than others.[116]

Next, gay identity must be supported and homophobia attacked through consciousness raising groups. Clark holds that small groups are the key to attitude changes.[117] Here community can be built as mutual support is given. "In Gay CR [Consciousness Raising] groups we can learn to laugh at the person who offers us tolerance or acceptance. That person is coming from a position of presumed superiority."[118]

At the same time, the values of being gay must be stressed. For gay men, other males are potential love partners, not competitors or enemies.[119] Since most gay people do not have permanent "marriages," they have more value for their day by day commitments. Also, among gays there is less gender stereotyping; people are more fully human.[120] Gays also have a deeper emotional capacity, more physical awareness and sensitivity.[121] In sum, while the heterosexual society is half, "We are whole."[122]

If "gay is good," why then is there the high degree of promiscuity in the gay community? Clark responds that gays have been programmed by the heterosexual culture where males are taught to compete for sex objects and pursue youth and beauty.[123] Over against this, he calls for relational sex where partners need to get to know one another by dating "before hopping into bed and reinforcing the instant physical attraction with an orgasm. . . ."[124] Clark advises sex with friends, rather than strangers, where sex is a friendly interaction to be offered to each other.[125]

Furthermore, Clark sees monogamy not as an identity, but as a technique for building trust. If it is not suitable for the relationship at any given time, it can do more harm than good.[126] The heterosexual marriage role model does not work for most gays.[127] As they relate to several sex partners, they should remember that the more one loves, the more capable one is of loving. Thus there is no reason for jealousy unless there is a feeling of love being withdrawn.[128]

In summary, for Clark, all of us are born gay—having the capacity to love a member of our own sex. Most of us, however, lose this capacity by society's deprogramming. Thus gays must not only affirm the natural basis of their homosexuality, they also must become the new cultural ideal.

The gay movement must raise the consciousness of gays by questioning society's basic dualistic and monogamous assumptions, and by creating groups for change. Then, there must be the reprogramming of gays into a new sense of their own dignity and worth.[129] Clark writes, "As the Blacks learned before us, integration is not possible until you cease to conform to stereotype and recognize your strength and the goodness of your identity." [130] Thus gays must come together, create their own culture and support systems, and then reapproach the straight world as equals. Quite likely this will help heterosexuals to discover that they too were "born Gay." [131]

What we have in Clark is a case for homosexuality based on the unproven assumption that we are all born with sexual feelings toward the same sex which are later socialized away.. We may ask, how does Clark prove that we are all bisexual? And even if we are, isn't the homosexual person in the same boat as the heterosexual person, having lost his attraction to the opposite sex? Isn't he just as "half-person" as the heterosexual who has lost his homosexual feelings? How then does this deficient homosexual person become the new cultural ideal?

In fact, an infant's sexual attraction for the same sex cannot be proven. That an infant is socialized into the object of his or her sexual attraction is clear. The potential is there but the defined target is yet to come. Thus to say that we are all born gay and that homosexuality is a gift at birth is a misnomer.

Moreover, if our sexual potential is undifferentiated then we need direction in employing it. Namely, we need God's order and God's goal as to where it goes. We are left in the dark here. Biologically we are born male or female. Biblically, as we shall discuss next, God has created us as male or female. Thus the cultural ideal and the most normal person should be the one who fulfills God's intention in creation.

Clark's view of promiscuity is absurd when he claims that the more people I love the more capable I am of loving. Does quantity make quality? Is love merely sexual adventure? Or does love include faithfulness, trust and care for the other person?

The value of Clark for our purposes here is to see the full weight of gay advocacy and the clear challenge which it brings to the church today. The gay question is not simply a matter of erotic preference. It is a challenge of the church.

In Conclusion

In our review of contemporary studies on homosexuality, several basic questions have surfaced.

First of all, who is a homosexual person? For Kinsey and Tripp, biology has the first word and this means that there are no neat homosexual/heterosexual categories. There is only a continuum. Many have homosexual experiences, most may have homosexual feelings at one time or another, all have a potential for homosexuality. Thus George Weinberg can speak of being homosexual for a minute, an hour, or a lifetime. Freud viewed all infants as bisexual and Clark even asserts that all are "born gay."

Here is a bold challenge to the Biblical understanding of persons created uniquely as male and female.

Next, what are the causes of homosexuality? As we have seen, for Clark it is nature itself that makes us gay and the heterosexual person has repressed his infantile homosexual feelings. For Hatterer and Tripp, however, there are many complex causes in the development of homosexuality which include parents, peers, and society. For George Weinberg the causes are simply unknown. If we are gay by nature, then God has made us so. If it is our socialization which forms sexual identity, however, then the causes are not necessarily natural or divine. We will need to evaluate this question carefully.

Finally, should homosexual persons seek change? For Hatterer, heterosexuality is still the norm. Tripp, Weinberg and Clark, however, abandon any such standard. If homosexuality is natural, it is idle or even perverse to change nature. Much of the frustration among researchers also comes in the failure by psychoanalysts and behaviorists to achieve significant change among people who are homosexuals. There is some ambivolence on the change issue, however, if all persons have bisexual potential. The very elasticity of Weinberg and Clark in defining who is homosexual keeps the question of change open.

All concur that society must abandon its homophobia. Weinberg lays part of the cause of homophobia at the door of the church. The Christian ideals of monogamy and procreation have excluded homosexuals from the mainstream of society. Clark offers a new ideal. It is the gay person who is "whole," who is the most complete in his or her sexuality. Heterosexual people are only half-people. Is this ideal, however, any less oppressive than the supposed oppression of a heterosexual ideal? Clark does not deal with this question. Is "wholeness" to be found in the isolation of one person alone—a "complete" homosexual? Again Clark fails to answer.

In summary, what we have in our four perspectives is some agreement and some disagreement. There is no single answer to be found in the observation of homosexual phenomena. Great variety creates much confusion. We turn then to the Bible in search of greater clarity on the issue. But, as we shall see, not even the Scriptures are immune from the severe challenge of homosexual advocates.

IV. The Biblical Teaching

When turning to the Bible for its understanding of homo-sexuality we must not jump in at any point which we choose. We must begin where the Bible begins: "In the beginning God. . . ." This becomes a critical point for us. The modern interpreters who claim that the Bible is not opposed to homosexuality *per se* start, not with the opening chapters of Genesis, "the beginning," but with the account of Sodom and Gomorrah. This is true of D. S. Bailey, Robert Treese, and John McNeill.[1]

But why not begin with Sodom and Gomorrah? Why begin with the creation narratives? The answer is simple and crucial. We begin with the creation narratives because there the meaning of human sexuality is given. For the Bible, homosexuality is always considered in relationship to human sexuality. It does not stand isolated or alone. To examine the specific texts on homosexuality without understanding the Biblical revelation on human sexuality is like trying to account for a tree without reference to its trunk or roots. Genesis, chapters 1-3, stand behind all else that the Bible says about God and man. To this we now turn.

Genesis 1-3: Creation and Fall

When we examine the opening chapters of Genesis we are confronted by some of the most sublime statements in all of the Bible. The grandeur of Genesis 1 and the graciousness of Genesis 2 stand in sharp contrast to the tragedy of Genesis 3.

While we have described these chapters as sublime, they are also a great battleground where frequent campaigns have been fought over the past century. The questions of the meaning of these texts, their relationship to the ancient world, their bearing on modern science and their relevance for theology have all been intensely debated. While we cannot continue these debates here, some preliminary remarks are in order.

Our thesis is that the opening chapters of Genesis are normative for proper Biblical interpretation and for Christian theology. In the canon, Genesis stands first as the book of "beginnings." Thus both synagogue and church have started reading the Bible here. Furthermore, the subject matter of the opening chapters of Genesis explains the origins of the universe, the relationship of God to mankind and the earth, the entrance of sin and the consequent disruption of life. In scholarly language, the opening chapters of Genesis contain aetiologies.[2] Von Rad notes that the union of primeval or universal history (Genesis 1-11) with sacred history (Genesis 12ff) answers the unresolved question in the opening chapters of Genesis about God's relationship to all people.[3] This becomes for him "the aetiology of all aetiologies" because the final purpose of God's work with Israel is "the bridging of the cleft between God and all mankind. . . ." [4] God promises to Abraham, "In you all the families of the earth shall be blessed" (Genesis 12:3). Furthermore, since the opening chapters of Genesis present the basic Biblical presuppositions, they speak for themselves. Sever these chapters from the Bible and the rest becomes problematic.

What then is the literary form and content of Genesis 1-3? Traditionally, scholars divide these chapters at Genesis 2:4b. The opening account of creation in 1:1-2:4a is described by Von Rad as "doctrine throughout."[5] Nothing in this section is without theological relevance as the focus is exclusively on God's words, work, order, commands, and regulations. Next, the account of creation and fall starting in 2:4bff is categorized as "saga" by Von Rad.[6] Jewett prefers to call it "narrative," because events are recounted in story form.[7]

These literary distinctions, however, must not lead to a separation of the texts, isolating their interpretation from each other. Genesis 2 now complements Genesis 1 by describing God's fatherly grace toward man and the account of the fall must be seen in light of the goodness of creation stressed in Genesis 1.[8]

Thus, we have, in the opening chapters of Genesis, concentrated theology and historical narrative. These chapters, however, do not view creation as an end in itself, but point forward to God's salvation and election which unfolds throughout the Bible.[9] Both creation and fall give the presuppositions and questions which remain to be answered. A good world made by God has been broken and disrupted. His judgment is pronounced and executed, yet His fatherly care is extended. How then will all this be resolved? We turn now to the first chapter of Genesis.

"In the beginning God created the heavens and the earth" (1:1). This simple, majestic verse begins the revelation of the God Who preexists His creation. He is therefore both transcendent over it and separate from it. The verb "create" (bara') contains the idea of creation out of nothing (ex nihilo), since it is unconnected to any account of building materials.[10] It also shows that God does not coexist with eternal matter (dualism), neither is He absorbed into it (pantheism). As Eichrodt writes, "Creation is *the free institution of a will which contains its Own norm.*"[11]

The first chapter of Genesis goes on to teach that God is not so much the first cause of creation as the source of *all* creation. He creates "the heavens and the earth." [12] Moreover, God speaks creation into existence, "And God said, 'Let there be light' and there was light" (1:3). By creation through the Word we learn that the world is not an emanation from God but a product of His will. Here the distinction between God and creation is defined. At the same time, as Von Rad notes, since creation comes through the Word of God, the world is susceptible to that Word. [13]

Creation both exists by God and is ordered by God. This order is reflected in the seven days of creation (1:3-2:2), the separation of light from darkness (1:3), the separation of the waters (1:6), the separation of the waters from dry land (1:9), the separation of day from night (1:14), the creation of vegetation according to its kind (1:11), the creation of living creatures according to their kinds (1:21, 24), and the creation of Man as male and female (1:27). Thus the theological thought of Genesis 1 moves from chaos to cosmos. As Von Rad concludes, "The actual concern of this entire report of creation is to give prominence, form, and order to the creation out of chaos (cf. the fundamental idea of 'separating')." [14]

The divine ordering is also teleological; God pursues His goal. Step by step through the seven days of creation we learn that there is purpose in the very structure of the cosmos. [15] All of this climaxes in the creation of mankind.

The crucial verses for our present study appear in 1:26-28:

[26]Then God said, "Let us make man in our image, after our likeness; and let them have dominion over the fish of the sea, and over the birds of the air, and over every creeping thing that creeps upon the earth." [27]So God created man in

his own image, in the image of God he created him; male and female he created them. [28]And God blessed them, and God said to them, "Be fruitful and multiply, and fill the earth and subdue it; and have dominion over the fish of the sea and over the birds of the air and over every living thing that moves upon the earth."

Several questions emerge from the text. Why does God speak in the plural, "Let us . . . "? What do "image" and "likeness" mean? What is the meaning of dominion? Why is Man created male and female? How does this relate to being made in the image of God? And finally, what is the relationship between creation and the ability to procreate? Does God simply create male and female in order to continue the race? Let us respond to each of these issues.

God's speech in the plural, "Let us make man in our image . . . " has been explained as address to the heavenly court, a plural of deliberation or reflection, the representation of a combination of powers in the deity, or a vulgar idiom.[16] Karl Barth sees the "Let us" as anticipating the Trinity. The plurality in mankind (male and female) made in the image of God, reflects the plurality in God Himself.[17]

As the passage begins, the announcement "Let us make man . . . " distinguishes this act of creation from all that has preceded it. Here is something special and unique. Human beings (represented by the collective noun "Man") are to be made in "our image, after our likeness." By "image" (selem) the Old Testament means an outward form, an actual plastic work, a duplicate, even an idol.[18] The immediate qualification of "image" by "likeness" (demūt), however, adds the idea of appearance or similarity.[19] Von Rad sees "image" made more precise by "likeness" with the meaning that this image is to correspond to the original.[20] He warns against spiritualizing the image of God into human personality or the ability to make moral decisions. The image embraces the whole person—body included.[21]

Eichrodt, however, holds that "likeness" qualifies "image" in order to exclude the idea that human beings are exact copies of God and to limit the concept to "similarity."[22] This view also receives support from Von Rad when he interprets the plural address "Let us make man . . . " as God's concealing Himself in His heavenly court to prevent the direct reference of the image of God to Himself.[23] For Eichrodt, since God in Genesis 1 is a purposeful person, human beings made in His image reflect personhood. They are self-aware, self-determined, open to the divine address, and capable of responsible conduct.[24] If this is dangerous spiritualizing then we should add Von Rad's corporeality, the sense of "wholeness," body and spirit. Since Genesis 1 is totally theological, however, Man must be seen in relationship to the self-revealing God who creates him. The nature of God determines the meaning of the image of God, not just a word study into the Hebrew meaning of "image."

Being made in the image of God, mankind is given a task in the world: dominion over the earth. The commission to rule is a consequence of the image. As Von Rad notes, "Just as powerful earthly kings, to indicate their claim to dominion, erect an image of themselves in the provinces of their empire, . . . so man is placed upon earth in God's image as God's sovereign emblem."[25] Mankind is to the world as God is to the universe.

After God's decision to create Man in His image (1:26), there is the event itself (1:27). The threefold repetition of the verb "create" adds solemn dignity to the act. Here we come to what Jewett describes as the first great surprise in the Bible.[26] Man is not just created for God and his neighbor, Man is created in the image of God as "male and female" (1:27). Thus the primal form of humanity is the fellowship of man and woman. Here we are at an essential point. God does not create Man alone, neither does he create man/man or woman/woman.[27] God creates Man as male and female and only in community together is the image of God seen upon the earth. Thus the old myths of the androgynous (bisexual or unisexual) Man are rejected and all ambiguity in the relationship between the sexes is removed. Man is created for another. That other is woman. Their relationship is ordered by God.

Therefore, while to be in the image of God means to represent God in dominion (1:26), it also means to be in fellowship as male and female. To be human is to share humanity with the opposite sex. For Jewett, ". . . to be in the image of God *is* to be male and female," [28] and to talk about Man as such is to talk about Man as man and woman. This is constitutional.

One further point must be made. God does not create mankind as male and female simply for the purpose of procreation, as McNeill asserts.[29] In fact, the blessing of procreation is quite distinct from being made in the image of God as male and female. Thus sexual ability is not an emanation or manifestation of the divine image as was held by the fertility cults.[30] For Von Rad, "It is therefore noteworthy that procreative ability is carefully removed from God's image and shifted to a special word of blessing." [31] There is no intrusion of sexuality into Man's relationship with God.[32]

One final note: all of creation is "good." We would assume this to be so because God is the creator. Yet throughout Genesis 1 the theme is repeated, "And God saw that it was good." The goodness of creation means that it conforms to the intentions of its Creator; it is perfect.[33] In Von Rad's phrase, "No evil was laid upon the world by God's hand. . . ." [34]

Here is revealed the transcendent, all-powerful God who speaks the world into existence. Here is God ordering His creation: chaos becomes cosmos; light is separated from darkness; waters above are separated from waters below; land emerges out of the oceanic depths; vegetation and living creatures appear and all procreate within their ordered limits. Finally, Man as male and female is created in the image of God. Now the climax is reached. The sexes too are ordered to represent the majesty and dominion of God in the world. Men alone cannot do this. Women alone cannot do this. We turn now to Genesis 2.

In the creation narrative starting in Genesis 2:4b we are greeted by many anthropomorphisms. God forms a single man from the dust of the ground and breathes into his nostrils the breath of life (2:7). Later the Lord God comes walking in the garden in the cool of the day (3:8). A hasty judgment might lead us to suppose that here in these pictures we have a more "primitive" narrative. For Von Rad, however, they express " . . . the candor and lack of hesitation which is only the mark of a lofty and mature way of thinking." [35] In narrative form, therefore, the same theological reflection continues as we have found in Genesis 1.

Nevertheless, while in Genesis 1 we are dealing with the whole universe, in Genesis 2 we are dealing only with the earth. The contrast in Genesis 1 is between chaos and cosmos. The contrast in Genesis 2 is between the desert and sown land, the garden. While in Genesis 1 mankind is the apex of the pyramid of creation, in Genesis 2 man is the center of the circle of creation.[36] Von Rad comments, "It is man's world, the world of his life (the sown, the garden, the animals, the woman), which God in what follows establishes *around man*; and this forms the primary theme of the entire narrative, *ādām adamā* (man-earth)." [37]

Man then becomes a "living being" when God breathes into him the "breath of life" (2:7). This life springs directly from God. Man is then placed in the garden to keep it (2:15) and to live under the authority of the Word of God, which is represented by the command not to eat of the tree of the knowledge of good and evil (2:16-17).

Now the incompleteness of creation is introduced when God says, "It is not good that the man should be alone; I will make a helper fit for him" (2:18). Thus, as in Genesis 1, Man is created for community. Von Rad sees the helper "fit for him" as being both similar and supplementary to him.[38] Since the animals fail to be "fit for him," man will only be fulfilled in association with another being like himself (2:19-20).[39] Thus as God has directly made the man, so he directly makes the woman from man, and in her he receives the helper who makes him a complete person. Once again, there is no bisexual or unisexual ideal here. Rather, there is a constitutional distinction in *the being of man* as woman is created from him, becoming "bone of my bones and flesh of my flesh" (2:23). Yet as Barth observes, "Were this creature only *like* him, a repetition, a numerical multiplication, his solitariness would not be eliminated, for such a creature would not confront him as another but he would merely recognize himself in it." [40] Thus this one "fit for him" is not another man, but a woman.

In the epilogue, "Therefore a man leaves his father and mother and cleaves to his wife . . ." (2:24-25), the application of the passage is made to marriage. Again the purpose of male and female is not fundamentally for procreation but for companionship, for community. But why do man and woman seek sexual union? The answer lies in woman being taken from man, for originally they were one flesh.[41] In their sexual union the "one flesh" is restored. Let us turn now to Genesis 3.

Here temptation comes to the first couple. It is the temptation to live beyond the limit of God's command (3:1). It is the desire to know "good and evil" and so be like God—to know everything.[42] First in question (3:1), and then in contradiction (3:4), the serpent leads the woman to rationalize her limitation (3:6) and fall (3:6). Her husband then immediately joins her and darkness descends.

The consequences for both man and woman are separation from each other, represented in covering their nakedness (3:7), and separation from God, represented by hiding among the trees (3:8).

In the resulting judgment man and woman now live in alienation and affliction. This alienation is both between them (3:16) and between the earth which is their home (3:17-18). Thus mankind now lives broken by rebellion, under God's judgment, cast from the garden, "East of Eden." Nature is no longer pure. Neither human beings nor their earth escape the curse. Identity, sexuality, and all of creation are broken, stained and judged by God. In Barth's phrase, this word of judgment is the next-to-last word which prepares us for the last word, the gospel of God's grace in Jesus Christ.[43] Here then in Genesis 2-3 we have theological history as narration: creation and fall prepare us for all that is to come.

In conclusion, we affirm that Genesis 1-3 is foundational for our understanding of God and Man, and our proper interpretation of the rest of Scripture.

Here we come to see that Man is created in the image and likeness of God as male and female. Male alone does not fully represent the divine image. Female alone does not fully represent the divine image. A community of simply one sex does not reflect God's intention for us or His character in the world.

At the same time, Man has been created as the pinnacle or center of creation to participate in God's ordering of the world. This includes the ordering of the sexes as male and female. To break this order is to create disorder, to turn from cosmos to chaos.

Furthermore, procreation is only secondary to the original intention of creating male and female for community in both Genesis 1 and Genesis 2. Therefore the unity of the two sexes cannot be overturned as merely a justification for their sexual relationship in creation which has now been transcended in redemption. Something more essential is at stake here: the reflection of the image of God through Man as male and female together. This unity of the sexes is then extended to their sexual relationship in the special command to be fruitful and multiply. Needless to say, a homosexual relationship is unable to fulfill that command. This leads us to suspect that this inability is a result of an improper ground. Man is designed to live together as male and female, nothing else fulfills God's will.

All creation, however, has fallen from God's original intention. Nature nowhere reflects the perfect will of God. The divine plan can never be established merely by observing human behavior apart from revelation. Chaos now threatens cosmos. Darkness has again descended. All is under the curse awaiting redemption.

Genesis 19: Sodom and Gomorrah

The account of Sodom and Gomorrah stands within the larger history of Abraham the father of the Hebrew people, through whom God's redemptive purpose begins. Venturing from Ur of the Chaldeans (Genesis 11:28) and accompanied by Lot, his nephew, Abraham journeyed to the land of Canaan under the command and blessing of God (Genesis 12:1-3).

In Canaan, Abraham and Lot separated with Lot moving to Sodom. In Genesis 13:13 we read, "Now the men of Sodom were wicked, great sinners against the Lord." This comment prepares us for the drama to follow where, after Abraham fails in his intercession for Sodom, the city is destroyed.

Traditionally, the destruction of Sodom and Gomorrah has been viewed as evidence that God abhors homosexuality. Thus, in English, to commit "sodomy" is to commit a homosexual act.

In Genesis, the fall of the two cities is preceded by God's decision to reveal His intention to Abraham (18:17). "Because the outcry against Sodom and Gomorrah is great and their sin is very grave . . ." (18:20), God goes down to see if the facts justify the case. Von Rad notes that the word "outcry" is a legal term expressing the cry of one who has suffered a great injustice.[44] Since the whole narration as it now stands is a legal account, after the outcry, the proceeding is opened. This includes Abraham's intercession (18:22-33), the preliminary inquiry into the case by the angels' visit to Sodom (19:1-11), and the confirmation of the "outcry" with resulting punishment (19:12-29).

For Von Rad, Abraham's intercession for Sodom introduces a new collective standard for divine judgment.[45] A minority of guiltless men will mean a reprieve for the whole city. Thus a small number of innocent people is more important to God than a large number of guilty. Continually agreeing to spare the city for their sake, He would rather save than punish. What then is the purpose of recounting Abraham's intercession? Von Rad replies, "After such willingness to forgive on God's part, everyone must consider the judgment on Sodom as really just." [46]

Genesis 19 then goes on to give the account of the "crime and punishment." The story is simple. Lot, Abraham's nephew, alone extends hospitality to the angelic visitors when they arrive at Sodom late in the day. After dinner the whole male population of the city, "all the people to the last man," surround the house and call to Lot, "Where are the men who came to you tonight? Bring them out to us, that we may know them" (19:5). Lot's response, defending the ancient law of hospitality, is to offer his daughters "who have not known man" instead. Establishing no restrictions, he says, "Do to them as you please . . . " (19:8).

The men of Sodom refuse, for Lot is only a sojourner, "and he would play the judge!" (19:9). They want what they want. But Lot and his people are rescued from the mob as the angels strike the Sodomites blind. Von Rad observes, "Sodom's sin is now established, the outcry of injustice done by the Sodomites (see at ch. 18.20) is fully confirmed. The preliminary inquiry into the case is concluded, the preparation for punishment begins." [47] And that punishment, we may add, is swiftly executed in the divine conflagration (Genesis 19:24-29).

Is the sin of Sodom homosexuality? Do the men seek to engage in homosexual *relations* with the angels, that is, in homosexual *rape*? Until recently the unequivocal answer was "Yes." With D. S. Bailey, however, this has changed.

The key question is: What do the men of Sodom want when they call upon Lot to bring out the angels, "that we may know them" (19:5)? Bailey answers that they are asking to "get acquainted with" the strangers. He writes, "The demand to 'know' the visitors whom Lot had entertained may well have implied some serious breach of the rules of hospitality." [48] Thus for Bailey there is no sexual meaning here for the verb "to know." Lot has exceeded his rights in Sodom as a sojourner and entertained foreigners whose intentions may be hostile.

Bailey defends his interpretation by pointing out that the verb "to know" (*yādhaʿ*) is used nine hundred and forty-three times in the Old Testament. Of these, in only ten cases does it denote sexual intercourse and then always heterosexual acts. [49] Furthermore, other Old Testament references to Sodom and Gomorrah never identify their sin as homosexuality. [50] For Jeremiah the sin of Sodom is adultery, lying, and an unwillingness to repent (Jeremiah 23:14); for Ezekiel it is "pride, surfeit of food, and prosperous ease" (Ezekiel 16:49-50). Bailey sees the homosexual interpretation of Sodom as a post-canonical Jewish reaction to Hellenization where homosexuality was particularly evident. He concludes, "Indeed it is not until we reach the late New Testament books, 2 Peter and Jude, that we find the sin of Sodom connected in any way with homosexual practices." [51]

What then should be said of Bailey's interpretation? In the first place, word count proves nothing, the context proves everything. That the demand of the men of Sodom to know the angels is a demand for sex in 19:5 is proven by the same use of the verb for sex in 19:8, "Behold I have two daughters who have not known man. . . ." It is also proven by the wider context of Genesis, for example in 4:1, "Now Adam knew Eve, and she conceived and bore Cain. . . ." Thus, even McNeill, who writes as an advocating homosexual scholar, admits that Bailey may have overstated his case. [52]

In the second place, the fact that the prophets refer to sins other than homosexual acts in Sodom and Gomorrah proves only that they were not faced with homosexuality. Thus, as good preachers, they applied these proverbially wicked cities to the evils of their own day. It may also be that there was a separate Sodom and Gommorah prophetic tradition as Von Rad proposes.[53] He concludes, "Sodom was always the example of greatest depravity that one could think of in Israel, but the notion about the particular nature of its sin was not always the same." [54]

In the third place, if the men of Sodom were only guilty of demanding the fulfilment of the law of hospitality by becoming acquainted with the angels, then we have no ground for the outcry against Sodom or its immediate destruction. Furthermore, if Lot kept the angels from fulfilling the demand of hospitality by going out to the men of Sodom, it is he who should have been judged, not them. Thus the outcry against Sodom becomes incredulous, and even McNeill admits this.[55] So, gay advocate Treese observes, "Whether Bailey's conclusions will, in time, gain widespread acceptance is somewhat problematical." [56]

What then is the sin of Sodom? The clear answer from the text is homosexual rape. The men of Sodom violated the unwritten law of hospitality by attacking the two angels. In so doing, they seek a sexual act contrary to Israel's morality (and, as Bailey has shown, also contrary to her neighbors).[57] Thus there are three aspects to Sodom's sin. The law of hospitality is broken, the distinction between angels and men is threatened, and the prohibition of sex between males is violated.

That Sodom is not a hotbed of homosexuality as such is clear from Lot's offer of his two daughters to substitute for the angels (this would have been no alternative for practicing homosexuals). The offer also points up the abhorrent crime of Sodom. Through his daughters Lot seeks to restore the divine order in human and male/female sexual relations, although he cannot prevent the rape. That he would sacrifice his daughters is one of the less commendable parts of the seamy narrative, although it may also represent Lot's extreme reaction to the horrendous desires of the men of Sodom.

Thus while the account of Sodom does not provide the Biblical basis for our opposition to homosexual acts, it assumes that basis: Man created as male and female. Here is illustrated God's judgment on violent, "unnatural" sexual acts. No wonder Sodom and Gomorrah become a picture of total corruption deserving God's righteous judgment throughout the Bible.

Leviticus 18:22 and 20:13: The Holiness Code

When we turn to the "Holiness Code" in Leviticus 17:1-26:46 we return to the world of Genesis 1, the transcendent, holy God ordering His creation and His people Israel. How are we to understand this code which contains the commandments against male homosexual acts?

Israel's law, according to Eichrodt, is communicated as the direct command of God. Thus we read in Leviticus, "And the Lord said to Moses, 'Say to the people of Israel'" (18:1).[58] In the law, therefore, the simple will of God is revealed without special pleading or qualification. Life is given high value as Israel's moral sense is deepened by the divine will. No special laws are given to the upper classes. All are equally accountable to the sovereign will of God.[59]

Moreover, the law establishes a higher tone to the relationship between the sexes.[60] Thus penalties for unchastity are more severely punished than in Babylonia. Also prostitution is illegal. Eichrodt observes, "If such a strengthening and refinement of the moral sense proceeds from the worship of Yahweh, then this God must be conceived as the power of goodness and the pattern of all human righteousness." [61]

The Levitical laws in the "Holiness Code" are priestly laws, "And the Lord said to Moses, 'Say to Aaron and his sons, and to all the people of Israel, 'This is the thing which the Lord has commanded' " (17:1-2). For the priests, God is unapproachable in His transcendent holiness. He communicates Himself, however, to Israel through His Law. Here the permanent divine order of life becomes manifested in the chosen people's history.[62] Thus the outward form of Israel's life is not a matter of indifference. For Eichrodt, it "effectively mediates the presence of the divine." [63]

Furthermore, the visible community is to be strictly distinguished from the surrounding pagan gods, their domain, and their immoral practices. Thus, "You shall not do as they do in the land of Egypt" (18:3). Israel, therefore, lives as a witness to the One God who has called her to reflect His character in the world, "Say to all the congregation of the people of Israel, You shall be holy; for I the Lord your God am holy" (19:2). The Israelites are to be God's sanctified people.

The specific laws against male homosexual acts are a part of the Holiness Code. Scholars are unable to date these laws, although Bailey notes the tendency now to treat them as pre-exilic.[64] The absence of any criticism of cultic worship leads Noth to see them also as pre-prophetic.[65]

In 18:22 we read, "You shall not lie with a male as with a woman; it is an abomination." This law stands in a complex of legislation devoted to prohibitions over "all non-permissible and especially unnatural sex relationships." [66] With the second person singular address, "You shall not" the law is the unqualified expression of God's sovereign demand.[67] What we have here is a simple prohibition against male homosexual acts.

Snaith, however, proposes to interpret this law in 18:22 in light of the previous one, "You shall not give any of your children to devote them by fire to Molech, and so profane the name of your God, I am the Lord" (18:21).

He notes that "by fire" is absent from the Hebrew text and that "to devote" (*lehacabir*) means "cause to pass through." [68] Thus, for Snaith, rather than this law prohibiting the fiery sacrifice of children to Molech, it really prohibits giving children to Molech as temple prostitutes.[69] So the verse should read, "You shall not give any of your children to pass through to Molech. . . ." Snaith then links this to the law against homosexual acts in 18:22. Both now reflect cultic sexual violation. To strengthen his argument, he points to the judgment in 18:22, "it is an abomination." Usually "abomination" (*To'ēbāh*) refers to idolatrous actions with other gods. Snaith concludes, "Thus homosexuality here is condemned on account of its association with idolatory." [70] Snaith's position, however, is open to several objections.

In the first place, Snaith has not proved that the law against homosexual acts should be interpreted in relation to the law against devoting children to Molech. The Molech law stands out of context with the other laws concerning sexual behavior in 18:19-23. In the parallel section to be discussed below (20:10-16) the law concerning Molech is absent although the law against homosexuality stands in a context similar to 18:19-23. This suggests that the law concerning Molech in 18:21 has found its way into this section and should not determine the interpretation of 18:22. Thus Noth calls the Molech law "striking," since it is out of context. He suggests that "it was only the key-word 'seed' (RSV "children") which brought this verse into the present context." [71]

In the second place, giving children to cultic prostitution in no way means homosexual behavior on their part. Such sexual action would contradict the fertility context of the pagan cults. As Bailey notes, "Homosexual coitus would be meaningless in the ritual of a fertility cult, with its exclusively heterosexual rationale, and there is no positive evidence that it was ever practiced in this connection." [72]

In the third place, the description of a male homosexual act as an "abomination" does not necessarily mean that the activity is more cultically associated with idolatry than any other sexual perversion. All such acts were committed before Israel arrived in the land by its former inhabitants, and thus have an idolatrous base (18:24-30). This does not, however, necessarily imply a cultic base.

After surveying Egyptian, Assyrian, Babylonian, and Hittite literature, Bailey concludes that the general attitude of Israel's neighbors was negative toward homosexual acts. The little evidence we have "plainly contradicts the opinion that homosexual practices were accepted without question." [73] Thus there is no reason to suppose that homosexual behavior endangered Hebrew morals and that the law against homosexual acts was designed to combat idolatry. The fact is that this law, "You shall not lie with a male as with a woman," clearly and simply prohibits male homosexual relations.

Thus Bailey concludes that this law and its counterpart in Leviticus 20:13 "relate to ordinary homosexual acts between men, and not to ritual or other acts performed in the name of religion." [74] The ground for this will be discussed after we have investigated the law in 20:15 to which we now turn.

Noth distinguishes the laws in Leviticus 18 from Leviticus 20 by the latter's pronouncing death upon the offender.[75] Thus we read, "If a man lies with a male as with a woman, both of them have committed an abomination; they shall be put to death, their blood is upon them" (20:13).

For Noth, the kernel of the code lies in Leviticus 20:9-21 where each law is a *mōt yūmat* statute. Noth renders *mōt yūmat* as, "he (the offender) is to be summarily put to death" or "is to be punished by death." [76] This judgment form stands between the apodeictic law, "Thou shalt," and the cauistic law, "If this, then that." It is, however, in itself apodeictic, that is, unconditional.[77] Apart from this and the plural, "*they* shall be put to death," the content is identical to Leviticus 18:22.

What then is the basis for this unequivocal condemnation of male homosexual acts? McNeill seeks to relativize these laws by finding their sociological necessity in the need of Israel to increase her population, the desire to preserve the family name (and immortality) in one's children, and the rejection of the male homosexual act as an act of domination which was used by conquering armies to humiliate their captives by treating them as women.[78] The deepest ground for the negation of homosexual acts for McNeill, however, is the connection between idolatry and homosexuality. He writes, "Whenever homosexual activity is mentioned in the Old Testament, the author usually has in mind the use male worshipers made of male prostitutes provided by the temple authorities." [79] There is, unfortunately, no evidence for this assertion as Bailey demonstrates. Furthermore, the use of males in a fertility cult is absurd.

What then is the ground for the prohibition of male homosexual acts? The answer must be found in Genesis 1. God has created Man as male and female. They are to be fruitful and multiply. This is His unchanging order for the sexes.

Bailey notes that an "abomination" is associated with idolatry in Leviticus and then extended to whatever reverses the proper order of things. Thus homosexual acts are an abomination not because of pagan cults, but because they reverse the natural order of sexuality. In so doing they manifest the spirit of idolatry, "which is itself fundamental subversion of true order." [80]

For the priests, God's divine order is established in

creation. Light is separated from darkness. Vegetation is brought forth "each according to its kind" (Genesis 1:11). Living creatures are created according to their kinds and Man is created male and female. Thus homosexual acts violate the order of creation and violate the divine will. As a result they are an "abomination." The ground of these laws then is theological and for Israel they cannot be altered.[81]

The Levitical code at this point is not some ancient, irrelevant law reflecting Israelite culture. It is not to be compared with other time-bound laws prohibiting the eating of pork or rabbit. It is the legal expression of God's will in creation and is therefore grounded in the fundamental assumptions of Biblical faith. To break this law is to revert to chaos. To keep this law is to live in harmony with God's will. There is no other option.

Judges 19: Gibeah

Judges recounts Israel's history after the death of Joshua (1:1) when there was "no king in Israel; [and] every man did what was right in his own eyes" (21:25). Thus the incident of homosexual rape at Gibeah in chapter 19 stands in the context of chaotic times.

Since the account of the Levite and his concubine in the "disgrace of Gibeah" has many parallels to Lot in Sodom, Von Rad does not rule out a "distant dependence." [82] Gray writes of a "variant tradition." [83] Boling, however, notes the contrast in the two narratives. While in Genesis Lot is only *accused* of judging the men of Sodom, in Judges the Levite actually does this and the theme is completely reversed.[84] Since the men of Gibeah are from the tribe of Benjamin, Saul's tribe, Bailey suggests that we have here an anti-Saul polemic.[85]

The outline of the story is simple. A Levite was sojourning in the hill country of Ephraim with his concubine (19:1).

Becoming angry with him, the concubine returned to her father in Bethlehem. After four months the Levite reclaimed her and was welcomed by several days of celebration hosted by her father. With the party over, and after a late departure from Bethlehem, the Levite refused to spend the night at Jebus (Jerusalem) because the city belonged to the Jebusites who were foreigners (19:11). Rather than taking this risk, he pressed on to Gibeah, since it was an Israelite city. There, however, the inhabitants who were Benjaminites refused to extend hospitality to him. Finally another sojourner, an old Ephraimite, took him and his company in (19:20-21).

While all were "making their hearts merry" that evening, base men of the city surrounded the house crying to the old man, "Bring out the man who came into your house, that we may know him" (19:22). The Ephraimite refused, describing their request as "this vile thing" (19:23). Instead he offered his virgin daughter and the Levite's concubine saying, "Ravish them and do with them what seems good to you, but against this man do not do so vile a thing" (19:24). So the Levite forced out his concubine and "they knew her, and abused her all night until the morning" (19:25). She then died on the doorstep and the Levite took her body and divided it into twelve pieces, calling together the tribes of Israel at Mizapah (20:1). War was then declared upon Gibeah after the Levite recounted his experience, asserting that the men of Gibeah surrounded the Ephraimite's house "to kill me" (20:5). Boling comments on this event, "The amphictyonic office is demeaned by the performance of the Levite who sets himself up as a judge and rallies the whole league to avenge his personal loss." [86]

The parallels between the Levite at Gibeah and Lot at Sodom are clear. In both accounts strangers who come to town are taken in by sojourners. The guests are then threatened with homosexual rape while their hosts defend them. Women are then offered as substitutes to the offenders. At Sodom the attack is thwarted by the angels' intervention. At Gibeah the attack is deflected by the concubine's ravishment. At Sodom the city is destroyed by God. At Gibeah a holy war is called by the Levite.

The point of the account of Gibeah is the erroneous breach of hospitality. The men of the city demand to "know" the Levite (19:22). Here is the call for homosexual rape. Instead they "know" the concubine (19:25) which fulfills the old man's offer for them to "ravish" his daughter and the concubine (ravish is a technical term for rape).[87] Thus the whole context is sexual and the verb "know" clearly means "to have sexual intercourse with." [88] Although the men of Gibeah demanded to abuse the Levite sexually (19:22) and do so to his concubine, he later reports that they had murderous designs on him (20:5), probably not wishing to admit their intention of homosexual rape.

The account of Gibeah, as is true of Sodom, assumes the sacred duty to provide hospitality and exposes the wickedness of those who are inhospitable. In both cases the sign of inhospitality is homosexual rape. That the men of Gibeah are not homosexuals is clear from their abuse of the concubine. Their intention, however, is vile, in part because of the proposed subjection of the Levite to sexual rape. Here both he and his sexual identity would be violated. This sin also clearly contradicts Genesis 1-2 and the Levitical Laws.

In conclusion, in Genesis 1-2 God creates Man as male and female. They are destined for each other and their sexual life is to be realized together in "one flesh." Thus same-sex acts are a violation of God's order in creation. This is expressed in the Old Testament by illustration (Genesis 19, Judges 19) and legislation (Leviticus 18:22, 20:13).

In both cases divine judgment against homosexual acts is clear. Sodom and Gomorrah are consumed in flames. Lying with a male as with a woman is an "abomination; they shall be put to death, their blood is upon them" (Leviticus 20:13). The divine order and the divine judgment prepare us to understand the New Testament. To this we now turn.

The Gospels

While it is true that Jesus never mentions homosexuality in the Gospels, it is also true that whenever he speaks about human sexuality he presupposes heterosexuality. Thus in Matthew 5:27-28 he applies the law against adultery to his disciples by warning them not even to look lustfully upon a woman (not a man). Furthermore, when arguing about the meaning of Moses's bill of divorce, Jesus appeals to creation, "Have you not read that He who made them from the beginning made them male and female, and said, 'For this reason a man shall leave his father and mother and be joined to his wife, and the two shall become one'? So they are no longer two but one. What therefore God has joined together, let no man put asunder" (Matthew 19:4-6). Thus Jesus asserts that God created Man as male and female, their sexual union produces "one flesh," and in this union it is God who joins them together.

In appealing beyond the divorce law of Moses, therefore, Jesus returns to God's intention in creation. This is constitutional. All else in human sexuality must be viewed from this vantage point if we are to follow the teaching of Jesus Himself.

The only alternative which Jesus offers to marriage is celibacy, making oneself a "eunuch" for the kingdom of heaven (Matthew 19:12).[89] Thus according to the Gospels he never entertains the idea of homosexual relationships. While it is true that this is an argument from silence, it is a strong argument. For example, Jesus also never defends the existence of God, he assumes it because it is an unchallenged presupposition for His life. The same, we hold, is true of Man created as male and female, and of sexual relationships being restricted to heterosexual marriage. But Jesus does more than simply assume this. He addresses it directly in Matthew 19:4-6, as we have seen.

Furthermore, Jesus probably never speaks to the issue of homosexuality because it was not a major problem for Palestinian Jews who retained their distance from the Hellenistic culture. Thus, as Bailey shows, the Rabbinical literature largely avoids the homosexual character of Sodom's sin.[90] This is similarly true of Jesus. When He refers to Sodom and Gomorrah He gives the cities a better fate on the Day of Judgment than those which have rejected His word and mighty works (Matthew 10:15, 11:23). He also employs Sodom and Gomorrah as symbols of carelessness before sudden judgment (Luke 17:28-30). He does not, however, speak of their homosexual violence. This contrasts greatly with Jewish literature from the Dispersion which was written during a time when the Jews were confronted by Hellenistic homosexuality. There Sodom and Gomorrah are notorious for their sexual sin.[91]

Thus both the Biblical foundation of God's creating male and female "from the beginning," and the absence of homosexuality among those addressed by Jesus determined his words on human sexuality in the Gospels. We turn now to Paul's letters.

Romans 1:26-27

Romans stands as the high point of Paul's exposition of the gospel. In it is revealed the free gift of God's righteousness (1:17). The epistle presents the massive themes of God's wrath, God's holiness, man's sin, Christ's grace, the new life in the Spirit lived out in the body of Christ. Traditionally, the letter has been divided into basic themes: justification (chapters1-5), sanctification (chapters 6-8), history (chapters 9-11), and the Christian community (chapters 12-16). What then is the context in which Paul writes to the Romans?

Having concluded his work in the East (15:23), the Apostle now turns his eyes toward Rome and Spain (15:24).[92] Before this new journey, however, he must take a collection of money to the saints in Jerusalem (15:25). After this task is completed, he anticipates coming at last to the capital of the Empire. There he will impart some spiritual gift to the church (1:11) and fulfill his obligation to bring the gospel to Greeks and barbarians (1:14-15). Thus he writes triumphantly, "I know that when I come to you I shall come in the fulness of the blessing of Christ" (15:29).

At the same time, Paul is both an Apostle of Confidence and an Apostle of Controversy. There are those Jewish Christians who hold that he has watered down his message by absolving the Gentiles from being circumcised and keeping the Mosaic law (see Philippians 3:1-11 and Galatians 5:1-6:16). Since Paul is unknown to the Romans by sight, he undoubtedly wonders if they will receive him warmly, or if the old questions of the law and Gentile freedom will once again become divisive. It is in this context then that he writes, paving the way for his arrival in Rome.

In contrast to the exclusiveness of the law, Paul presents the inclusiveness of the gospel. It is addressed to both Jew and Gentile, and is adequate for both (1:16). Both are therefore to welcome each other with Christ's welcome (15:7). Through the gospel all are called to live together in the one body of Christ (12:1ff). Since the gospel reconciles both Jew and Gentile to God and to each other, they must display its reality in the church and in the world. We turn now to Paul's specific passage on homosexuality.

Romans 1:26-27 stands in the wider context of the revelation of God's righteousness (1:17) and God's wrath (1:18). While God would have us stand before Him as "not guilty" in the righteousness of Christ, we will only be ready for this when we hear the thundering "no" of His righteous judgment against our rebellion, our sin, our depravity, our unbelief, our idolatry, our hard-heartedness, our false motives, our selfish, lustful immoral lives.

Paul begins with God's indictment of us, "For the wrath of God is revealed from heaven against all ungodliness and wickedness of men who by their wickedness suppress the truth" (1:18). By God's wrath Paul does not mean a violent outburst of anger, but the moral judgment of the wholly righteous God upon our immorality. Here it is asserted that God's wrath is *revealed*. Where then do we see this revelation? Paul's reply is that God's wrath is made visible in human sin and depravity. This is expressed in the threefold "God gave them up . . ." (1:24, 26, 28). God gives us up to our corruption. God lets sin run its course as He steps back and we "do our own thing." The cesspool of our evil and poison darkens as history progresses. All idealistic illusions of evolutionary progress, the improvement of our moral nature, and our own ability to save ourselves are shattered by the wrath of God.

This wrath is righteous because God has made Himself known through creation and conscience to the Gentile (1:19-20; 2:14-16), and through His law to the Jew (3:2). Both Gentile and Jew, however, because of their sinful nature have been unable to live up to God's light. The immoral unbeliever and the moral, but hypocritical, believer are both the objects of divine judgment since " . . .all men, both Jews and Gentiles, are under the power of sin" (3:9).

Why this word of divine judgment? Why this stern indictment? Why God's "No"? The answer is clear—to drive us to despair; to call us into accountability before our only true judge; to turn the spotlight upon the cancerous evil which grips us; to smoke us out of our hiding; to bring us before the bar of divine justice. As Paul expresses it, God's wrath against our sin is in order that "every mouth may be stopped, and the whole world may be held accountable to God" (3:19).

Here our sin is exposed. Here our facades are stripped away. Now our games are over. We can no longer rationalize our sin. There is no escape, no exit. We are before the Holy God. We are undone. We are silent. We are without excuse. Caught red-handed in our sin, we are only dismayed and dumb. We are dead!

Now and only now are we ready for the gospel. Into the darkness God's light has broken. The "No" of wrath is countered by the "Yes" of grace. Crushed into the dust, we are raised from death into life. Here is good news. "But now the righteousness of God has been manifested apart from law . . . the righteousness of God through faith in Jesus Christ for all who believe" (3:21-22). Again, it is God's turn not ours. He comes to us in Christ with His own gift of righteousness. "Not guilty" is His surprising word. We, the guilty, are set free. We, the sinners, are forgiven. We, the unrighteous, are pronounced righteous. All of this is accomplished as Christ dies upon the cross, bearing our sin and God's wrath, that we might be called into a new life in Him. As Luther says, God's holiness and God's love kiss in the cross. When we come to Christ by faith alone, as in marriage, we receive all that He is and He receives all that we are. We receive His righteousness; He receives our sin, and we are restored into the divine presence. In Christ there is a smile upon God's face. Our judge becomes our justifier. The Father welcomes us home. There is a divine heart in the universe, and that heart is love.

It is in this exposition of God's wrath and man's sin preparing us for the gospel that Paul treats the homosexual acts referred to in 1:26-27. When we give up the true knowledge of God we create substitutions and we become idolaters (1:23). Thus we are the objects of His judgment as God gives us over to our sin. And when we no longer know who God is, we no longer know who we are because our identity is to be found in Him. This loss of identity is well illustrated and documented by homosexual acts. Not knowing ourselves, we do not know how to use our sexuality. Paul writes,

> [26]For this reason God gave them up to dishonorable passions. Their women exchanged natural relations for unnatural,[27] and men likewise gave up natural relations with women and were consumed with passion for one another, men committing shameless acts with men and receiving in their own persons the due penalty for their error.

First of all, Paul shows that homosexual behavior is a result of God's judgment upon human sin, "God gave them up . . ." (1:26). Furthermore, homosexual behavior now includes women as well as men (this is the only place in the Bible where lesbians are mentioned). Thus it is universal. Homosexual behavior is also described as the exchange of "natural relations for unnatural" and the result is that those who engage in them bear in their own persons "the due penalty for their error." All of this seems clear and simple. This passage, however, has not gone unchallenged. Questions of interpretation, context, and theology have all been raised. To these we now turn.

The problems of interpretation center on whether Paul describes female homosexual acts here and what he means by natural and unnatural.

Bailey entertains the thought that women exchanging natural relations for unnatural could mean unnatural heterosexual acts.[93] He concludes, however, that this is

unlikely because of the clear context of male homosexual
acts in 1:27, and the parallelism between the two verses
seen in the adverb "likewise," "and the men likewise gave
up natural relations. . . . " [94] We agree with Bailey.

It is more difficult to understand Paul's meaning in the
words natural and unnatural. By "unnatural" does the
Apostle claim that homosexual acts are the perversion of
nature? Or does he mean that homosexual acts are simply
against his religious and cultural heritage? [95] In other
words, by "nature" does Paul mean the "customs" of people or the "essence" or structure of reality?

For McNeill, the Apostle does not make a sharp distinction between natural law and social custom.[96] Thus in
our passage, on the one hand, he may mean that when
men and women exchange natural relations for unnatural,
the heterosexual goes beyond his or her own sexual appe-
tites to indulge in new pleasures. Thus "natural" or "cus-
tomary" sexual use is abandoned. On the other hand,
Paul's reference may be, according to McNeill, "to the
'nature' of the chosen people who were forbidden by Levitical law to have homosexual relations." [97] Moreover,
Paul tends to fuse the concepts of custom and essential
nature and therefore McNeill concludes, "Both interpretations are probably valid." [98] What, however, can we
learn from the Apostle's use of "nature" elsewhere in Romans?

Since the Gentiles who follow their conscience are described as doing "by nature" the law in 2:14 and are called
uncircumcised "in their true nature" in 2:27, i.e., really
Gentiles,[99] Paul quite certainly also means the essential
order of things by "nature" in 1:26-27. Thus the sexual
violation of what is natural refers not to relative customs
but to the Levitical code against homosexual acts which
in turn is based on Genesis 1, God's order for the world
as we have seen. So Barrett comments, "In the obscure

pleasures to which he [Paul] refers is to be seen precisely that perversion of the created order which may be expected when men put the creation in place of the Creator. That idolatry has such consequences is to Paul a plain mark of God's wrath." [100]

Under the questions of interpretation then, we conclude that Paul speaks of both male and female homosexual acts, and sees them as contrary to God's intention in creation and, thus, in violation of the Old Testament law. We turn next to the questions of the context and intention of 1:26-27.

George Edwards seeks to prove that 1:26-27 is not normative for Paul's theology because it is merely traditional Jewish polemic employed by the Apostle to trap the religious "Boaster" (2:17) who denounces the sins of others, but fails to see his own sin.[101] That Paul is using traditional material from Jewish preaching is seen by the parallels betwcen Romans 1:18ff and the *Book of Wisdom*, a late Jewish tract. This proves that he is engaging his Jewish audience on its own ground. Thus 1:18ff, the revelation of the wrath of God, is a prelude to 2:1ff where its intention is fulfilled in the exposure of this "Boaster," "Therefore, you have no excuse, O man, whoever you are when you judge another . . . because you, the judge, are doing the very same things." Paul's purpose, then, is neither to attack Gentile homosexuality nor to give ethical instruction to the church, but to place the Boaster under God's judgment. In the history of exegesis, however, the text has had the opposite effect, placing the church in a boasting relationship to the homosexual person. What can be said of this argument?

In the first place, Edwards's demand that 1:26ff be taken in its context is crucial since the context must control its meaning. But what is that context?

Edwards discovers it in 2:17, in the "Boaster." Thus

for him 1:18-32 serves 2:1ff in bringing the Jew under condemnation for his hypocrisy. Is this, however, the proper context? We hold not. Paul's indictment of the Gentiles in 1:18ff cannot be made into stereotyped Jewish polemic used simply to catch the Jew, since Paul's intention is to preach the gospel equally to Jew and Gentile (see 1:14-16). If anything, Paul's focus is on the Gentile rather than the Jew. He has, however, a universal obligation embracing both. Thus in 3:9 he gives his conclusion, "I have already charged that all men, both Jews and Greeks, are under the power of sin." Thus for Paul, the accusation against the Gentiles in 1:18ff is not absorbed into his attack upon "the Boaster." It stands on its own merits.

In the second place, in 1:18ff itself is Paul lacking serious theological intention and merely echoing stereotyped apologetics such as appear in the *Book of Wisdom*? Historically speaking, we must remember that Paul is a Jew. He embraced much of Jewish theology as his own.[102] However traditional the position in 1:18-32 is, can we seriously think that Paul would not have agreed with it heartily? The denunciation of idolatry and resulting immorality is too apparent in his other letters to need cataloging. In other words, the judgment that Paul's thought here is "traditional" cannot mean that for him it is not true. Furthermore, when 1:18-32 is compared with *The Book of Wisdom* the deeper and more profound theology of Paul emerges clearly. While *The Book of Wisdom* only mentions homosexuality in passing in a vice catalogue (14:26), Paul gives an extended exposition of homosexuality, not simply as a result of idolatry, but as a clear manifestation of the wrath of God.

The attempt to eliminate 1:18-32 from Paul's doctrinal foundation violates the whole context of Romans. Even if, however, the Apostle only writes this section to catch the Boaster and bring him under conviction, does this mean that it is not true? If the argument leading to the conclusion is not true, how then could the conclusion itself be true? Whether the polemic is traditional or not, only if it is true will it result in driving the Boaster to despair.

At the same time, however, it is clear that Paul's purpose in 1:18-32 is not merely to catch the Boaster, but to announce God's "No" on the rebellion of Gentile and Jew against the true knowledge of God. Paul presents his universal indictment to bring us all to despair before the judgment of God, in order that we may be ready for the gospel. Finally, having dealt with the questions of interpretation and context, we turn to the theological question.

For Bailey, a fundamental distinction must be made between homosexual perversion and inversion.[103] A heterosexual person engaging in homosexual acts is a pervert. A "constitutional" homosexual person who has never desired the opposite sex is an invert. Bailey asserts that Paul knows nothing of this modern distinction which would have been unintelligible to him.[104] Furthermore, if the Apostle had understood this, Tresse supposes, he would have chosen other illustrations of sexual idolatry rather than homosexual acts.[105] In other words, a homosexual person acting out a same-sex relationship would be acting naturally and therefore not be a sign of disorder.

Thus for McNeill, scripture can only be held to condemn homosexuality if it can be interpreted as condemning the actions of an invert. He asserts, "To such situations, however, it can hardly be said that the Bible addresses itself. . . ."[106] Interpreting 1:27 then, McNeill sees the use of the aorist participle, "and the men likewise gave up (aphēntes) natural relations . . ." as representing the conscious choice of the pervert, and thus contrary to his sexual identity.[107] This means that for McNeill, Bailey and Treese, Romans is not relevant to our modern theological discussion which centers on inversion, the "constitutional" homosexual person.

While we will postpone a full response to this problem for our final conclusions two points are in order here. In the first place, for Paul, as McNeill holds, nature means not only "custom" but also the law of the Old Testament based on the order of creation. If this is true, then the Apostle cannot be ruled out of the modern theological discussion. He, like Jesus, has a sense of "the beginning," and his attack on homosexual behavior presupposes that beginning. If there is some other beginning, such as natural evolution, then Paul may be irrelevant. If Genesis 1 is *the* beginning, however, then Paul's attack on homosexual acts is both right and theologically sound, regardless of whether he understood inversion or not. In other words, Paul does not simply observe nature as a modern biologist and then reach his conclusions. Paul begins as a theologian by hearing the Word of God that Man is created as male and female.

In the second place, Paul sees the consequences of homosexual acts not merely as isolated violations of one's heterosexual identity. He writes that those who commit them receive "in their own persons the due penalty for their error" (1:27). This suggests that Paul sees a tragic homosexual lifestyle as a further sign of God's wrath. Homosexual persons bear in themselves the result of God's judgment. This is the result of more than a lapse into same-sex activity.

In conclusion then, in 1:26ff Paul represents homosexual acts as a sign of God's wrath against rebellious mankind. Giving up the true knowledge of God, we have become idolatrous. No longer knowing who God is, we no longer know who we are. Thus we no longer know how to relate to each other sexually, and we no longer understand the proper function of our sexuality. God's intention for "natural relations" is voided, and those who violate that intention already bear the marks of judgment in their tragic persons.

Paul then drives to his conclusion that God's decree is death for those who commit homosexual acts (1:32). Here the Apostle is consistent with the Levitical laws and the account of Sodom and Gomorrah. We turn next to I Corinthians.

I Corinthians 6:9

Paul writes his first letter to Corinth to respond to a report from Chloe's people (1:11) about chaos in the church and to answer a letter from the Corinthians (7:1).

The congregation is torn with dissension. There is division over leadership (1:12) and legal incest (5:1). Members are suing one another in civil courts (6:1), while some still visit prostitutes (6:15). Moreover, the church asks Paul questions about marriage (7:1), eating meat offered to idols (8:1), spiritual gifts (12:1), and the collection of money for the saints (16:1).

Overall, the Corinthians are tempted to adopt a message and lifestyle which is contradictory to the gospel. They are offended by the foolish cross (1:18) and are in danger of denying the resurrection (15:1ff). They seek a powerful, spiritual existence in this world and favor the gift of tongues as its ecstatic expression (14:1ff). Thus Paul writes from Ephesus (16:8) to call the church back to the gospel (15:1-3) and to reorder its life based on his example, since he is their father in the faith (4:15). We turn now to 6:9-10 where the Apostle warns,

[9]Do you not know that the unrighteous will not inherit the kingdom of God? Do not be deceived; neither the immoral, nor idolaters, nor adulterers, nor homosexuals, [10]nor thieves, nor the greedy, nor drunkards, nor revilers, nor robbers will inherit the kingdom of God.

In these verses we have traditional Pauline exhortation

given through a catalogue of vices (compare Romans
1:29-31 and Galatians 5:19-21). Conzelmann notes that Paul
draws here on set tradition,[108] and Barrett sees this
list as closely paralleling similar summaries in pagan and
Hellenistic-Jewish sources.[109]

The theme of inheriting the kingdom of God is repeated
in the beginning of verse 9 and in the conclusion of verse
10. Again, for Conzelmann, this is not particularly Pauline,
but common Christian expression bearing a high apocalyp-
tic sense.[110]

The exhortation, while a bit broken from the immediate
context of some Corinthians suing each other (6:1ff), serves
as a warning and a call which bridges to the next subject
of those who visit prostitutes (6:12ff). Thus the elaboration
of sexual sins in the vice catalogue prepares for what
is to follow.

But at the same time as Paul warns about the unrighteous, he refreshes the church with a reminder of God's
work. Thus after the list of vices he writes, "And such
were some of you. But you were washed, you were sanctified, you were justified in the name of the Lord Jesus
Christ and in the Spirit of our God" (6:11). In summary,
then, what is clear to us is that Paul condemns several
sins, warns that those who practice them will be excluded
from God's kingdom, and yet is confident of God's grace
in Christ. What is not clear, however, is the meaning of
the two Greek words rendered "homosexuals" by the Re-
vised Standard Version.

For Conzelmann, Paul makes the sins of sexual immorality specific by introducing both the passive (*malakōs*
—"pervert, effeminate") and the active (*arsenokōites*—
"Sodomite") homosexual person.[111] Barrett renders
the words "catamites, sodomites" and notes that they
mean the passive and active partners in male homosexual
relations.[112] Bauer sees *malakōs* as used "of persons

soft, effeminate, especially of catamites, men and boys who allow themselves to be misused homosexually," [113] and *arsenokōites* as "a male homosexual, pederast, sodomite." [114] These definitions of both words, however, have been challenged.

McNeill, following an unpublished study by John Boswell, claims that *malakōs*, meaning "soft," is used here of those "morally weak, or lacking in self-control." [115] He concludes that there is no justification for applying the term to homosexuality since in patristic Greek it never bears that specific meaning. Its normal use refers to any form of immorality. [116]

Furthermore, for McNeill, *arsenokōites* is never the same as "homosexual" in classical, Biblical, or patristic Greek. [117] It is used in the second century in the *Apology of Aristides* as "an obsessive corruptor of boys," [118] and in the sixth century *Penitentiale* of Joannes Jejunator, Patriarch of Constantinople, for, most likely, anal intercourse. McNeill concludes, "It is possible that the author attached to the compound a meaning like 'male prostitution.' " [119] What can be said of this?

To render the first word, *malakōs*, as simply "immoral" is to remove it from its specific context. Paul has already spoken of the "immoral" at the beginning of the vice list using *pōrnoi* which means "fornicators," or those prone to sexual immorality. [120] To use *malakōi* in this sense, therefore, would be redundant. Furthermore, it is immediately preceded by "adulterers" and immediately followed by *arsenokōitai* ("male prostitues" or "sodomites"). Thus, in the context of the series it must be taken in a sexual sense. As Bailey notes, "There is little doubt concerning the sexual reference of *malakōi*. . . ." [121] Now it makes more sense to see the "soft" or "effeminate" as connected with "sodomites" rather than with "adulterers." Thus the context leads us to favor the word as referring to the passive partners in homosexual acts, especially as McNeill admits that the following word, *arsenokōitai*, probably refers to those engaged in anal intercourse.

To establish that *arsenokōitai* is a technical term for "male prostitutes" from a sixth century A.D. source is precarious, to say the least. Also, to have Paul address one professional category of sexual perversion here, when all the other terms are more generally applicable, is again out of context. Why would the Apostle single out "male prostitutes" when he is referring to "idolaters, adulterers, thieves, greedy, etc.?" While *arsenokōitai* by the sixth century may mean "male prostitutes," here it certainly has a wider reference, "male homosexuals, sodomites"— literally, "male bedmates for males." [122] Thus Bailey concludes that *malakōi* means those who give themselves to passive homosexual acts and *arsenokōitai* means those engaging in active homosexual acts. [123] Tresse also concurs with Bailey, as do we. [124]

In conclusion then, Paul offers the Corinthians a traditional warning against the vices that would keep them from the kingdom of God. Included among those sins are passive and active homosexual behavior. The Apostle's point, however, is not just a warning. He immediately turns to his triumphant report, "And such were some of you. But you were washed, you were sanctified, you were justified in the name of the Lord Jesus Christ and in the Spirit of our God" (6:11). Thus former homosexual Corinthians had found a new life in Christ and at the heart of that new life was the moral resolution of God's forgiveness and His indwelling Spirit.

Here is a startling word of hope in the gospel. God's order in creation is for us to live as male and female before Him and with each other. This order determines our proper sexual relationship. Although sin has distorted this God continues to pursue His purpose for us.

The negative side of that purpose is seen in His legislation against the violation of His order in homosexual acts. It is also seen in His judgment of Sodom and the manifestation of his wrath through the perversion of natural sexuality as seen in Romans.

The final word, however, is God's grace which can forgive us and free us to once again fulfill His will for our sexuality. This the Corinthians had experienced and this is the promise to every generation of believers. Sin, chaos, and judgment do not have the last word. Christ does. Let us hear Him!

I Timothy 1:10

This "pastoral" epistle is one of the few Pauline letters written to an individual. While Timothy is its recipient (1:2), I Timothy also deals extensively with matters for the church in Ephesus (1:3).

The first issue faced in the letter is that of false teaching by "certain persons" (1:3, 6). This teaching includes "myths and endless genealogies" and speculations (1:4; 4:7) with a misapplication of the law (1:7). Not only is there doctrinal confusion, but some have also departed from the faith, being deceived by false spirits and "doctrines of demons" (4:1). This includes asceticism, both in food and sex, and a radical dualism in "what is falsely called knowledge" (6:20). Ethical chaos is the certain result (1:19).

Theological and moral confusion are also producing disorder in the functioning of the church. Thus Paul gives instruction for various official responsibilities including bishops (3:1-7, 5:17-22) and deacons (3:8-9, 12-13).

That Paul is the author of I Timothy has been the traditional position of the church. This is upheld by some modern commentators,[125] although others give the letter to a later hand.[126] Regardless of the question of authorship (although we opt for Paul), I Timothy is canonical and therefore authoritative.

The specific verse mentioning "sodomites" (1:10) is a vice catalogue similar to that found in I Corinthians 6:9. In I Timothy, however, the context is different. Here Paul is teaching about the proper use of the law. It is laid down not for the just but for the "disobedient, for the ungodly and sinners, for the unholy and the profane. . . ." This then leads the Apostle into a more specific list of sinners who are to benefit by the law. It is for "murderers of fathers and murderers of mothers, sodomites, kidnapers, liars, perjurers, and whatever else is contrary to sound doctrine . . . " (1:9-10).

Dibelius and Conzelmann note that the list of vices is structured by the Ten Commandments and is a Hellenistic transformation of Jewish ethics.[127] The seriousness of the sins, such as murderers of fathers and mothers, is due, not to contemporary events in the church, but to the formal style of gross sins in "Tabular form."[128] Thus we have here an early Christian catalogue adapted from Hellenistic-Jewish exhortation (parenesis).[129]

Kelly argues, furthermore, that the list follows the Decalogue and relates "immoral persons" (pōrnois) and sodomites (arsenokōitais) to the Seventh Commandment against adultery, "which was interpreted as embracing sexual vice in all its forms. . . ."[130]

The meaning of "sodomites" has already been discussed in our study of I Corinthians 6:9. Once again, we take it to designate males having sex with males.

For Paul here, the prohibition against homosexual acts is supported from the Old Testament law. The proper use of the law then is to expose sin (1:8). It is noteworthy that the Apostle understands the Ten Commandments to be violated by homosexual acts. This gives strong evidence for the position that behind Paul's theology stand the Holiness Code and the orders of creation in Genesis 1-2.

Not only does Paul specifically prohibit homosexual acts in Romans 1:26-27, I Corinthians 6:9 and I Timothy 1:10, he also always presupposes that heterosexuality is the norm when speaking of human sexuality. Thus in I Corinthians 7, the Apostle covers a wide range of sexual issues: the married, the unmarried, mixed marriages, divorce, celibacy, the betrothed and widows. Nowhere, however, does he seek to give positive orders for the sexual behavior of homosexual persons, although there were those formerly homosexual in the Corinthian congregation. Nowhere does Paul recommend loving, faithful, monogamous homosexual "marriages." This is not merely an argument from silence. Paul refuses to recommend homosexual relationships in any form because for him they are sinful. Formerly some of the Corinthians engaged in such acts (6:9) but now they have been washed, sanctified and justified. Homosexual relationships are not merely to be made responsible, they are to be cleansed away as the homosexual person is converted and conformed to Christ.

In Ephesians 5:21-33 again Paul speaks of marriage. In the marriage relationship husbands and wives are to submit mutually to each other (5:21). They then are to act out that submission by wives being subject to their husbands (5:22-24) and by husbands loving their wives as Christ loved the church and gave Himself for her (5:25). Only together in their mutual relationship do they mirror the relationship between Christ and the church in their marriage (5:32). Thus both the unity of the sexes in mutual submission, and the diversity of the sexes in husbands and wives are upheld. There is no analogous application of this teaching to homosexual couples, the diversity of the sexes being destroyed by homosexuality (compare also I Corinthians 11:3-16).[131]

Thus Paul teaches both the positive intention of God in creating Man as male and female and the negative result that homosexuality is a perversion of that intention.

In this teaching he is both consistent within his letters, consistent with Jesus' teaching, and consistent with the Old Testament. No other conclusion is tenable.

Jude 7

Jude identifies himself in 1:1 as "a servant of Jesus Christ and brother of James." Traditionally, this James has been taken to be "the Lord's brother," which would make Jude another brother of the Lord. Boobyer finds no decisive case against this conclusion.[132] Bigg follows Clement of Alexandria in proposing that Jude rejects the title of "the Lord's brother" by humbling designating himself as a servant of Christ Jesus. He then calls himself only "James's brother." [133]

The letter itself is written to warn the early Christian communities of false teachers who are guilty of "licentiousness and deny our only Master and Lord, Jesus Christ" (verse 4). They probably represent a combination of early antinomianism and gnosticism. Bigg sees the churches addressed as mainly Gentile.[134] Boobyer, however, suggests Gentile proselytes from Jewish synagogues,[135] and Leahy proposes Jewish Christians in the Diaspora.[136] This would account for the references to the Old Testament and the Apocryphal writings.

Of interest to us is Jude's reference to Sodom and Gomorrah in verse 7. This is used along with the judgment of Israel in the wilderness and the punishment of rebellious angels to illustrate God's certain destruction of those who "defile the flesh, reject authority, and revile the glorious ones" (verse 8).

How does Jude understand the sin of Sodom and Gomorrah? They "acted immorally (ekporneūsasai) and indulged in unnatural lust (sarkos eteras)." Or as William Brownlee renders verse 7, "they went fornicating and chasing after the wrong kind of flesh." [137]

That fornication is mentioned here by Jude clearly makes the sin of Sodom and Gomorrah something other than the mere violation of hospitality; it is sexual in nature. McNeill, however, argues that the homosexual element is incidental. For him the real emphasis is on the sexual incompatibility of angels and men.[138] In this he is following Bailey who finds similar themes in the pseudepigraphical literature of intertestamental Judaism.[139]

The "unnatural lust" (*sarkōs etēras*) or "wrong kind of flesh" would refer then to the attack upon the angels by the men of Sodom. It is interesting here that Jude sees two violations of the divine order: men seeking after angels and a homosexual act. "Fornication" now includes homosexual as well as heterosexual sin.

In II Peter 2:6-10 there is a similar use of Sodom and Gomorrah. Lot, however, is explicitly mentioned and, as Bailey notes, II Peter substitutes for fornication and lusting after "strange flesh" the general accusations of lasciviousness and lawless deeds.[140]

The importance of Jude is that it gives a clear Biblical witness to the sexual nature of Sodom and Gomorrah's sin. This is consistent with what we have already discovered in Genesis 19.

Furthermore, Jude sees the judgment of that sin as not merely a temporal destruction. The cities have undergone "a punishment of eternal fire" (verse 7). Thus the condemnation of Sodom and Gomorrah is comparable to the judgment that a male homosexual act deserves death in Leviticus 20:13 and Paul's conclusion in Romans 1:32 that those who do such things deserve to die. Fortunately, that is not the last Biblical word on homosexuality. Although all sinners deserve to die, Christ has died for all, "that those who live might live no longer for themselves but for Him who for their sake died and was raised" (II Corinthians 5:15).

V. The Theologians

Writing in 1955, D. S. Bailey terminated his study of homosexuality and Christianity with the Middle Ages because in his words, "it does not appear that the tradition has undergone any significant alteration since that time. . . ." [1] Since Bailey, however, things have already changed. To gain perspective on these changes we will examine the theological works of Karl Barth, Helmut Thielicke, and John McNeill. Barth's position toward homosexuality is traditional. Thielicke represents a moderating view and McNeill calls for the full acceptance of advocating homosexual persons into the church. What then are the theologians saying?

Karl Barth

In his *Church Dogmatics* Barth devotes four volumes to the doctrine of creation, including a lengthy exegesis and exposition of Genesis 1-3, [2] and an extended discussion of Man as male and female. [3] In the final volume he also devotes one page of fine print to homosexuality, which is clearly only a passing theological issue for him. [4]

For Barth, God is revealed as the Creator. To Him are owed the reality, content, and order of heaven and earth. [5] But how are we to know this? Certainly not by reason or scientific observation or even by starting to read Genesis. Such knowledge is never naturally accessible. God the Creator and the creation by His Word are only known through faith in Jesus Christ. Because of human sin the Creator is now known through the One who has reconciled the creation to Himself. Thus the Bible must be interpreted from its center: Jesus Christ; we must read the Old Testament through the New Testament. Since the whole Bible speaks figuratively and prophetically of Christ when it speaks of creation, Barth concludes, "What is said in prospect of Him can be understood only in retrospect of Him." [6]

From the unity of God and man, reconciled in Christ, we learn two things. In the first place, God is not alone. He acts in the created sphere where Jesus is Lord. In the second place, man is not alone. He is a creature who is the object of divine grace. [7]

What then is creation? It is God's first work. It is not redemption, "although both reconciliation and redemption have their presupposition in creation and to that extent already begin with it." [8] And what is the purpose of creation? Its meaning is found in the institution of the covenant of grace: God has called man to be His partner. [9] Thus the aim of creation is the history of that call and in that sense creation belongs to history. [10]

Creation itself is the external basis of the covenant, making it "technically possible." [11] The internal basis of the covenant, however, is the free love of God. That God desires a partnership with man is seen in the covenant between the Father and the Son who in His incarnation bears human nature and represents all of creation to the Father.

Turning now to the opening chapters of Genesis we have three alternatives for their interpretation. The first is to view them as meaningless. In this case, the understanding of creation will be left to our own metaphysical or scientific genius. Thus every age will view creation according to its own assumptions and the relationship between God and man "will necessarily fall victim to a corresponding variety." [12]

The second alternative is to separate creation from the Fall and see in it a philosophy or cosmology of creation. This, however, is improper since creation and history belong together. From the beginning man is set in a covenant of grace, and thus nature has no separate reality apart from it. [13]

The third alternative is to see creation and history together. For this reason Barth speaks of "a history of creation" which takes place in time. [14] He also describes creation as "prehistorical history" because it is a history which cannot be deduced and compared apart from faith, adding, however, that "this does not mean that it ceases to be genuine history." [15] Thus Genesis 1-2 contains creation history rather than creation myth and lays the basis for God's covenant with man.

In Genesis 1 Man is the summit of creation. In the call to share in God's Sabbath rest (Genesis 2:2-3) we find that the goal of creation is grace. [16]

Man is also made in the image of God. As such he both coexists with God and is independent from Him. The image of God is not an attribute of Man but Man himself. Barth writes, "He would not be Man if he were not the image of God." [17]

The plural, "Let us make man in our image . . ." (Genesis 1:26) means that in God Himself there is both relationship and differentiation. [18] Thus God creates Man as a being in relationship and differentiation. [19] As God exists in Himself as an "I" and "Thou" so Man exists in himself as an "I" and a "Thou." The basic *form* of humanity then is fellow-humanity; "Man is in fact fellow-human." [20]

What more can be said about that form? Only that

Man exists in relationship and differentiation as male and female. Thus Barth writes, " . . . we cannot say Man without having to say male or female and also male and female." [21] This is the only structural differentiation in Man. He exists in this concrete duality, not as an abstract human being beyond sexual polarities.[22] Thus Barth concludes, "Man can and will always be Man before God and among his fellows only as he is man in relationship to woman and woman in relationship to man." [23] Together man and woman also become the great paradigm of all that is to take place between Man and God in the history of salvation.[24] God makes a covenant with Israel as God has called Man into a covenant with Himself.

Furthermore, the sexual relationship between man and woman must have no independent life apart from their total humanity as male and female. Barth sees the divine command to be "fruitful and multiply" as the "friendly Word of God." [25] The command both limits and sanctifies physical sexuality.[26] Barth comments, " . . . coitus without coexistence is demonic." [27]

While Man is made male and female, Barth refuses to stereotype their cultural roles. This does not mean, however, that masculinity and femininity are illusions. It is before God that they are understood as both diverse and distinct.[28]

In the creation account in Genesis 2:4bff Barth stresses the freedom that man has as God brings the gift of woman to him. "Apart from this act of human freedom, the supreme and final gift of God would not be what it is." [29] Man must will to conform his humanity to the woman who is both similar and dissimilar to him.[30]

Furthermore, for man to recognize his duality with woman, God must enter again. Thus, "He creates not only the I and Thou, man and woman, but also their mutual relationship." [31] The climax of the account, however, is not that man says "Yes" to woman but that he says "Yes" to God in the presence of woman, thus giving the glory to God.[32]

In the fall, Man made in the image of God as male and female is not overthrown. The image remains "even in face of the total contradiction between it and the being of man." [33] Thus God's will stands although everything that belongs together has disintegrated, everything created in a definite order has been thrown into confusion.[34] It is from this understanding of creation that we can appreciate Barth's opposition to homosexuality.

To begin with, God does not create a second man for the first man. God seeks a being resembling him but different from him. Barth asserts, "If it were only like him, a repetition, a numerical multiplication, his solitariness would not be eliminated, for it would not confront him as another but he would merely recognize himself in it." [35] Thus it is necessary that the second being be a woman; like man and unlike man at the same time.

Thus Barth sees the denial of the other sex or the desire for some transcendent bisexual ideal as a "lofty movement of escape." [36] To reject that one is a male in relationship to a female is to become "semi-sexual." This type of consciousness has been impregnated with the magic of mysticism and gnosis precisely because it is a flight from concrete humanity as "fellow humanity." [37] We must not seek to transcend our sexuality. Bisexuality is the desire to embrace the myth of wanting to be whole alone. It is the sin of *hybris*, pride.[38] There is, however, no such thing as a self-contained male or female life. Barth concludes, "We should never want to know better than God the Creator whose will in this respect is simple and clear." [39]

Turning specifically to homosexuality, Barth sees it as a physical, psychological, and social sickness, "the phenomenon of perversion, decadence and decay, which can emerge when man refuses to admit the validity of the divine command. . . . " [40]

The refusal to recognize God leads to the failure to appreciate Man as male and female. From this comes an ideal of a masculinity free from woman and a femininity free from man. The result is a corrupt and physical desire "in a sexual union which is not and cannot be genuine." [41]

The early stages of homosexuality, however, may appear beautiful and spiritual. Barth is unimpressed. He responds, "What is needed is that the recognition of the divine command should cut sharply across the attractive beginnings." [42]

The real perversion of homosexuality is trying to be human in oneself as a sovereign man or woman. This then "is the place for protest, warning, and conversion." [43] Man can only be human with woman. Barth concludes, "In proportion as he accepts this insight, homosexuality can have no place in his life, whether in its more refined or cruder forms." [44]

We turn now to a more moderate position.

Helmut Thielicke

Thielicke and Barth share the common assumptions of Man created by God as male and female. For Thielicke, this sexual differentiation is a Biblical axiom apart from which it would be impossible to express what it means to be human. [45] Thus Man is created to live as a Thou to a Thou in mutual dependence.

In the creation of woman from man's rib, therefore, Thielicke finds the parable that they are destined for each other. [46] Endorsing Barth's view of Man as "being in fellow-humanity," he sees masculinity and femininity as a "polarity constitutive of man as such." [47] When God determines to create a helper fit for man in Genesis 2:18, Thielicke holds that the Hebrew text requires the meaning, "I would make him a helper as his opposite." [48]

Furthermore, the Fall does not obliterate the primeval order of male and female.[49] Thielicke writes that the "duality of Man remains as a constant within the history of salvation. It was ordained in creation and continues to endure through the crisis of the Fall, except that here it becomes a *disturbed* relationship." [50] Thus when Jesus speaks of marriage as God's making the two one flesh "from the beginning" he connects the order of creation to the order of redemption.[51] It is only a false eschatologizing which says that Christ transcends our sexual polarities, and seeks to evade in a visionary way our "being-in-the-world." [52] This kind of theology produces an abstract concept of "Man" stripped of all reality.[53]

For Thielicke, however, the image of God as male and female is not only expressed in the polarity of the sexes. It also represents our unmediated relationship to God. Here our sexual distinction loses is force. The equality of the sexes also breaks through the old hierarchy of superiority and subordination with a new personal mutual responsibility.[54] This for Thielicke, however, does not void living together as male and female in this world. It is in this context then that he examines homosexuality.

Homosexuality must be understood in relationship to God's creation of Man as male and female. The homosexual must see himself in disparity with the polarity of the sexes and still bound by that polarity.[55] Thus the Christian may not view homosexuality as a simple variant of nature.[56] It is, rather, a habitual or actual distortion or depravation of it,[57] which then justifies speaking of homosexuality as a "perversion." By this, however, Thielicke does not imply a moral depreciation. He only means that in every case homosexuality is not in accord with the order of creation.[58] "Abnormal" would also be an appropriate word in the same sense as disease, suffering, and pain are also not in accord with creation. Thielicke writes, "this points, then, to the hidden connection between the Fall as a disordering of creation and the pathological changes in existence in the world as a whole." [59]

The homosexual predisposition is no different than all fallen human nature. Thus, for Thielicke, "there is not the slightest excuse for maligning the constitutional homosexual morally or theologically." [60] Here a clear distinction must be made between the homosexual's condition and its actualization in concrete sexual acts.[61]

When Thielicke turns to the Biblical passages on homosexuality he demands that they be interpreted in accord with the purpose of the gospel.[62] Thus he sees the Levitical laws against male homosexual acts (18:22, 20:13) as reflecting cultic defilement. This opens the question as to their relevance for those who are under the gospel. Turning to Paul in the New Testament, Thielicke entertains the idea that the Apostle may only be attacking the sexual disregard for one's neighbor, "a particular *way* of homosexual behavior (possibly analogous with adultery, polygamy, etc.)." [63]

Furthermore, the passage in Romans 1:26ff is only a particular illustration of the theological point that a vertical disorder in our relationship with God results in a horizontal disorder in our relationship with man. Therefore the Apostle's exposition of homosexuality is not a separate theological statement. For Theilicke, this "gives us a certain freedom to rethink the subject." [64] This he proceeds to do.

Since homosexuality is in violation of God's intention in creation, what must the Christian homosexual do? To begin with, he cannot affirm or idealize his status.[65]

He must be willing to be treated therapeutically in so far as it may be possible to bring him back to the created order.[66] If, as a "constitutional homosexual" he is largely untreatable, then he must accept his condition as we must accept any incurable ailment.[67] It is then a divine dispensation, "a task to be wrestled with. . . ." [68] Furthermore, it is irrelevant to demand celibacy of a constitutional homosexual person since this is a special gift and calling based on one's free choice.[69]

What, however, if the incurable homosexual Christian cannot practice sexual abstinence? Can he have a sexual relationship with a member of the same sex? For Thielicke the answer is a guarded, "Yes."

The question now is whether the homosexual person is willing to structure the man-man relationship ethically.[70] Thus Thielicke writes, ". . .the homosexual has to realize his optimal ethical potentialities *on the basis* of his irreversible situation." [71]

Such a sexual relationship may not be carried on in the open since it violates the order of creation.[72] It will also be faced by clear temptations. These include the absence of a supporting order of marriage and resulting propensity toward promiscuity, the inability to find a partner in the regular, open contacts of society, and the burden of living "in the closet," acting like a hypocrite with a constant fear of discovery. Thus Thielicke is not optimistic over the chance for a permanent partnership. The homosexual person is left to realize relative ethical values in a questionable framework.

Thielicke criticizes Barth's placing the sickness, perversion, decadence and decay of homosexuality on the same level because "sickness" is ethically neutral.[73] He also sees the homosexual encounter as a search not simply for oneself but for the totality of the other person. Thielicke comments, "He who says otherwise has not yet observed the possible human depth of a homoerotic-colored friendship." [74] In distinguishing between homosexual acts and the "constitutional" homosexual person, Thielicke has joined the more contemporary issues of homosexuality. We turn finally to the position of full acceptance by the church of advocating homosexual persons.

John McNeill

Father John McNeill, a Jesuit priest, presents the case for a reversal of the traditional Christian understanding of homosexuality. For him, the old structural approach to sex based on natural law, dogma, and a certain view of the Bible must be rejected.

The crisis of the church in dealing with homosexuality is that time-honored answers are not functional. The goals of changing a homosexual person to a heterosexual person, or of sexual abstinence if that fails, are not an option for most people. In light of this, the whole Christian position must be reworked.

Rather than a structural view of sex, McNeill calls for a relational view of sex. For him, the Bible teaches that a sexual act which is a true expression of human love is morally justified. [75] Thus in contrast to the legalist tradition of natural law (Stoic), [76] the Bible presents a "personalist" understanding of human sexuality. [77] For this reason the interpretation of Genesis 1 which sees man as living in the image of God only as male and female must be rejected. McNeill bases this upon the observation that because of God's radical gift of freedom, our sexual identity-image is formed culturally rather than given to us. Thus it is a human rather than a divine creation. If this is so, then for McNeill, "Theologians who absolutize the man-woman relation as the 'divine image' in man are guilty of raising a human creation to the level of an idol." [78] Thus, by implication, both Thielicke and Barth in particular are to be rejected.

The task of theology, then, is to liberate us from structured sexual-identity images. God's goal for us is not to live as male and female, but "to fashion cultural identity images that make it possible for human beings to achieve the fulness of a true personal relationship of sexual love in the process of conforming to the images provided by culture." [79] The form of love does not matter; the content is everything. [80] In an ethical sexual relationship there must be growth and reconciliation, mutual support and fulfillment. [81] The goal now is the wholeness and full development of the person.

That McNeill is interpreting the Bible from a certain point of view becomes clear when he notes that moral theologians used to rely upon an objective biological function in order to understand human nature. Today, however, "the modern theologian tends to seek his primary evidence for what is true to human nature from psychological and sociological data." [82] The social sciences teach us that human development is dynamic rather than static; sexual orientation comes from free cultural adaptation rather than biological instinct, and the ethical question now is to search for goals to guide that free cultural development. Here then, for McNeill, whatever is loving and personally fulfilling in sexual activity is ethical regardless of its formal structure; heterosexual or homosexual.

This leads McNeill to a reexamination of the Biblical data on homosexuality. The sin of Sodom (per Bailey), could be the failure of hospitality, [83] or the passage may reflect a polemic against the "unnatural sex vices" of Israel's neighbors in their idolatrous cults. [84] Likewise, the Holiness Code in Leviticus reflects the condemnation of homosexual acts only as they are related to idolatry. [85] Following Thielicke, McNeill asserts that Paul only uses homosexual sin in Roman 1:26ff illustratively,[86] and never treats the homosexual condition as such.

Since the Bible does not distinguish between the pervert and the invert,[87] it does not understand the "permanent psychological position" of the homosexual.[88] Thus it does not immediately apply to us. The only certain word of condemnation in the Scriptures is directed toward perverse homosexual activity by heterosexuals.[89]

After examining the Christian tradition in its understanding of human sexuality, and weeding out Stoic influences, McNeill concludes that procreation is not the only goal of sexual relationships. The affirmation of "natural" contraception in the Catholic church undercuts the view that all homosexual acts are wrong since their goal cannot be procreation.[90] Furthermore, the sex act must not be judged by the biological function of the sex-organs, since we are not bound by nature but have great personal responsibility.[91] McNeill then concludes, "The call of the gospel to man is not one of conforming passively to biological givens; rather, that call is to transform and humanize the natural order through the power to love." [92]

For homosexuality to be a part of the divine plan, however, it must serve God's purpose in the world. What then can we perceive that to be? McNeill offers several answers. Firstly, the homosexual will help to build a more humane society by delivering us from stereotyped sex-identity images. These images in the male/female polarity are only partial while the homosexual has a more whole sense of himself.[93] Rather than being a male to be completed by a female, the homosexual can see himself as total and his love for another as an equal love.[94] McNeill even asserts that since homosexual love "escapes the debilitating effects of the heterosexual identity images, perhaps it has a better chance to form the basis of a genuine interpersonal love." [95]

The homosexual can break the stereotype of the dominating male,[96] and reduce the need to identify masculinity with violence.[97] Therefore, the homosexual is freer to see himself as a servant in society, taking roles currently thought of as "feminine." [98] In the church, the homosexual with a passive and receptive attitude will be more open to prayer and the reception of revelation.[99] While Christ was not a homosexual, McNeill mentions Jung as observing that the qualities attributed to Him are the striking characteristics often attributed to homosexuals.[100]

While painting this ideal picture, McNeill admits that often homosexuals do not fulfill these goals and actually imitate in an exaggerated way the worst features of heterosexual images, in, for example, sado-masochism.[101] He also backs off his idealistic picture in an apparent contradiction when he writes, "No more important fact needs to be established than the fact that the homosexual is usually no less varied than his heterosexual counterpart, for the most part no better and no worse." [102] Then, seeming to abandon his whole project, he concludes, "The true fact is that there is no such being as a homosexual, any more than there is such a being as a heterosexual: there are human beings who happen to be, relatively, heterosexually or homosexually inclined." [103] If this is the case, the whole discussion of God's purpose in homosexuality becomes obscure. Besides, the cultural relativity of McNeill's homosexual ideal is manifest.

What, finally, is the church's ministry to homosexuals? For McNeill, the first goal should be the traditional one of heterosexual adjustment. This is simply because of our homophobic culture and church. There is less pain in being a heterosexual.[104] The second goal, especially in counseling, is the need to establish whether the individual is truly a homosexual. McNeill quotes Hettlinger approvingly that "no one in the student age range has reason to conclude that homosexual urges, however strong, are either basic or permanent." [105] For the constitutional homosexual, where abstinence is no option, then again a loving, fulfilling sexual relationship must be the goal. McNeill concludes, "If true Christian and human love can exist equally in a homosexual or in a heterosexual context, then there is no a priori basis for a moral choice between these contexts." [106]

While it would be erroneous to view just these three theologians as wholly representative of the trends in theology over the past fifty years, nonetheless, a few comments on their work would be helpful to us in understanding the recent discussions on homosexuality. The most significant aspect of the movement from Barth to Thielicke to McNeill is the growing weight which is given to the "facts" proposed by the social scientists on the nature of homosexuality. The second point which deserves comment proceeds from the first. Because of the effect of modern social scientific research on both Thielicke and McNeill we find them using the term "constitutional" homosexual. The impact of this acknowledgement on Thielicke and McNeill is substantial as it leads Thielicke to accept homosexuality as a static human condition for some (although still out of the will of God) and it ultimately causes McNeill to abandon starting with the Bible in favor of modern research.

Are we watching the further enlightenment of the church or are we seeing the deterioration of Biblical authority? Have the social scientists uncovered a phenomenon about which the Bible is silent (as McNeill would have us believe), and must we now read the Bible in light of that discovery (as Thielicke proposes)? Barth clearly holds the most consistent theology on the issues. The existence of homosexuality must be understood in light of God's revelation of the purpose of human sexuality in Genesis 1-2. Man has fallen, yet Christ has come to redeem us and to restore us. Because of this we must affirm heterosexuality as the norm and call all believers in the gospel to uphold that norm.

VI. Conclusion

Where Shall We Begin?—A Definition

Foundational to a study of homosexuality is the formulation of a clear understanding of what a homosexual person is. We need a working definition as the first step in coming to our conclusions on the question of homosexuality.

"Static" or "dynamic"? These are terms for two positions which have emerged from our investigation. To distinguish between them is essential. As we shall see, the choice of either determines the final understanding of homosexuality. Let us first make a brief summary of both approaches and then follow with some comments upon them.

The static definition of homosexuality holds that a homosexual is a person who has a dominant or exclusive erotic preference for the same sex and is capable of acting out on it; a sexual preference which is a fixed reality in that person's life. Thus, in this sense, homosexual persons compromise a "third sex" which lies beyond heterosexual masculinity or feminity.

This "static" position on homosexuality tends to see human nature as predetermined, fixed and unchanging, fitting neatly into clear categories. As a result of this a distinction is often made between a static homosexual and a situational homosexual. For example, a situational homosexual might be someone who, after having a series of

homosexual experiences in a prison, reverts to heterosexuality when released. This person's homosexual activity
is seen to be a result of his situation—it does not reflect
his fixed sexual preference. In short, this person is a static
heterosexual who has participated in homosexual behavior.

Those who hold to the static definition of homosexuality
tend to create dualistic categories. There are perverts—
heterosexuals engaging in homosexual acts; and there are
inverts—those with a static homosexual identity. To try
to change a homosexual person to a heterosexual is to
incur the wrath of the proponent of the static definition.
Indeed, such manipulation of a "static homosexual" is
an attack upon nature or, worse, a violation of the sacred-
ness of human personality. It might even be tampering
with God's creation!

Those defining homosexuality as a static condition also
tend to look upon homosexual persons as uniquely fulfilled.
Gay advocates idealize them. They become the new cultural norm, those most in touch with the full range of
their humanity or even those most approximate to the
ideal of Christ Himself.

On the other hand we have the "dynamic" definition
of homosexuality. This position views human sexuality as
a continuum between two abstract poles labelled "homosexual" and "heterosexual." (The word "dynamic" is used
in contrast to static to communicate that sexual preference
is flexible and changing). Virtually all of us fall somewhere
in between the extremes, being more or less homosexual
or heterosexual. Furthermore, many advocates of this
viewpoint claim that all of us have homosexual potential
which is waiting to be activated. Heterosexuality is no
longer the natural or moral norm, but rather it is the
statistical norm because research shows more people to
be actualizing their heterosexual potential.

Here the distinct, careful, clear-cut categories are gone

and relativity claims the field. There is no discussion of "static nature" or of a "fixed sexual preference," but rather only of an erotic desire that has a same-sex target. Thus for Weinberg, one may be a homosexual for an hour or a day as well as for a lifetime.

Where do we stand with these two definitions? For us, the dynamic definition of homosexuality seems to be more to the point. Kinsey has shown that millions of adult males have had extensive homosexual experience— yet they have not adopted homosexuality as a lifestyle or identity. This only illustrates for us that human beings are the least instinctual of all creatures, having almost unlimited freedom for growth and change. We establish our neat, rational categories and then slip right through them.

Moreover, in our freedom, tasks which are pre-programmed for lower primates are ours to be learned. These include our gender identity as male or female, our gender roles as the cultural expression of that identity, and our sexual preferences. To be sure, such learning is complex and mysterious, but it is learning nevertheless, and we can go in a multitude of different directions because of it.

Before we decide upon a final definition of a homosexual, we need to clarify our acceptance of the dynamic category we looked at above. What we mainly accept within that position is the notion that human sexuality is learned behavior. Any suggestion that we embrace the dynamic category *in toto* would be false, and we will outline our belief in the static dimension of sexuality in greater detail later on.

For us then, a homosexual is a person who has a dominant erotic attraction to members of the same sex. This attraction normally leads to behavioral fulfillment. By using the word "dominant" we are opting for the dynamic definition. Rather than speaking of "static homosexuals" or "inverts," we prefer to speak simply of homosexuals as persons who have learned to meet their needs by targeting their sexual desires toward the same sex.

Since human nature is malleable, adaptable, and changing, we are constantly learning and relearning. Moreover, if we all have homosexual potential, then we all have heterosexual potential as well. The question for us then is not how we are programmed, or what our static sexual preference is. The central issue is what we are choosing and affirming to be our sexual role. What conscious and unconscious choices are we making—or are being made for us? Here is the heart of the issue. Human sexuality is dynamic, not static. But if this is so, and if we are in need of making these choices, then we are in need of light to know which choices to make. In other words, if the dynamic nature of our sexuality allows us to choose and to learn is there also any static dimension of our being which guides us in the way to go?

The Starting Point—Revelation or Observation

In evaluating homosexuality and its relationship to the Christian faith a crucial decision must be made about one's starting point. Where does the evaluation begin? Do we start with God's revelation of His divine will or with man's observation of the human condition? The choice between revelation or observation as a starting point is one of monumental consequences which cannot be overlooked in this discussion.

If biology takes precedence (Kinsey), or if nature is all we have (Tripp), or if psychology and sociology must tell us about who man is (McNeill), then when we go to the Bible our principles of selectivity have already been established. For example, since, according to McNeill, the social sciences have the first word for the moral theologian, man must be seen in a "personalist" context. Thus human beings are solely dynamic and there is no static dimension to their sexuality. Already, then, McNeill leads us to be suspicious of the structural categories of Genesis 1 where man is ordered as male and female.

Furthermore, since the social sciences hold no absolutes, the Biblical absolute against homosexuality must be neutralized. This is accomplished by explaining away most of the scriptural texts as so culturally and historically determined that they do not bear authority for us today. Those that remain are rejected because they presuppose a heterosexual committing homosexual acts, a "pervert," rather than an "invert" or "static homosexual."

In other words, if the Bible doesn't fit our categories, it is the Bible which must bend. When the social sciences have the first word, the Bible may have the second word, but the social sciences will be the final arbiter as they select what of the Bible is relevant for us. More often than not we see that our conclusions are born in our presuppositions.

In summary then, if we start with a personalist psychology, this will determine our outcome. The goal of man's life will be humanistic—the development of his full potential. The thinking behind this is as follows: God has made us to be fulfilled persons, therefore whatever fulfills us is the will of God. If we start with God, however, His will determines our outcome. The goal of our life will be His glory rather than our own. There is an entirely different rationale: God has made us for Himself, therefore the will of God fulfills us. The goal of man's life is God's call and God's gift. This may or may not meet a modern psychological interpretation of a fulfilled man as perceived by the movement for human potential. Jesus indeed loved and cared for people, but He also never married. He lived an itinerate life, preached the radical Kingdom of

God, was in constant conflict with the authorities, was rejected by even his closest friends, and then executed by Rome. This isn't quite our vision of the fulfilled life.

The Bible—God's revelation of His will—must be our starting point. His truth and His means of human fulfillment do not always meet our expectations. We can never depend on observation leading us to divine order. Rather, we must let the revelation of God guide us in our observation of the world around us.

Where Shall We Begin?— Human Sexuality or Homosexuality

As we are building the foundations for our final conclusions we face another decisive crossroad. We have defined homosexuality and stated that the Bible will hold the key to understanding the human condition—but where do we start within the Bible? Do we go immediately to the specific texts on homosexuality? Here again is a major choice—another watershed, another turning point, as we shall see. Our choice is to start with Genesis, and we will do so for two reasons.

In the first place, the opening chapters of Genesis are foundational for all Christian theology as we showed in earlier chapters. Most Christians who think through their faith accept the early part of Genesis as setting the necessary presuppositions both for the Bible and themselves as they come to understand God as Creator, the world as His creation, Man made in the image of God, man as fallen, nature as now corrupt and all that follows. If we accept Genesis 1-3 on these points, what right do we have to reject its clear teaching that God has created Man as male and female to live in community together?

In the second place, not only is this understanding of Man fundamental for the Old Testament, it is affirmed by the New Testament. In the Gospels Jesus rejects Moses' divorce law given for our hard hearts because "it was not so from the beginning" (Matthew 19:8). For Jesus, "the beginning" is God's creation of Man as male and female to be joined in marriage as "one flesh." Thielicke observes that here the order of creation is wedded to the order of redemption; Jesus fulfills the Old Testament and in His work He restores God's initial intention for us given in creation.

If we ask where the Bible begins its discussion of human sexuality the answer is clear: Genesis 1-3. And if we ask where to begin our evaluation of homosexuality again the answer is clear: Genesis 1-3. For in Genesis 1-3 we find the clear exposition of God's intention for His created beings—Man as male *or* female, Man as male *and* female (Barth). Thus when we get to the specific texts on homosexuality we will approach the issues as their authors did—presupposing the notion of Man as male and female as recorded in Genesis. It is an error to begin an analysis of homosexuality in the Bible with the specific texts on homosexuality because that is not where the Bible begins its discussion of sexuality. The Bible deals with the topic in Genesis 1-3, and this is also where we will begin.

As we begin this section of our conclusion we must first define some terms which are crucial to our understanding of homosexuality. The first is gender identity: what you perceive yourself to be—male or female. The second is gender role—the manner in which you act out on your gender identity. This varies widely and is determined both by culture and family. Lastly, there is sexual preference—the choice of what the object of your sexual desires is, either the same or opposite sex.

The question which lies before us now is the nature of human sexuality; here the terms static and dynamic become valuable again.

While we affirm that human nature is dynamic, and that sexual preference is learned, at the same time we insist that there is a static reality behind our gender identity. God has created us male and female; it is He who calls us to our gender identity, He who wills our sexual duality. The full image of God will only be seen, not simply by man or by woman alone, but by Man in community as male and female. We are called to be male *or* female and male *and* female. We have no real choice in the former, as we are created male or female. We do have choice in the latter—but how?

Our gender is determined for us. We are biologically either male or female; in this there is no option. Our gender identity, however, according to modern research, is learned. For example, if we take a child with indistinct male sex organs at birth, and tell him that he is a girl, call him "Nancy," treat him like a girl, he will grow up to be a girl, until puberty throws him into chaos. Unless we have a clear gender identity, we will live psychologically tragic lives. Gender identity is at the heart of our individual identity. Every person alive must be able to say, "I am a boy," or "I am a girl." As Money and Tucker write, " . . . your identity—is the essence of you, and at the core of it lies your sense of yourself as male or female, your gender identity. It is the kingpin of your identity, the anchor of your emotional health." [1] And they conclude, "It is practically impossible for a person to develop any sense of identity at all without identifying as either male or female, and the gender identity gate locks firmly behind." [2]

Clearly, an infant with normal sex organs begins to receive his or her gender identity moments after birth. This is then reinforced through lifelong learning. The duality of gender identity, male or female, is based on genital differentiation. Both psychology and biology agree—we are male or female. In this they support the Biblical revelation that God creates us male and female to reflect His image in the world.

Now while gender identity is more distinct, clear, and immediately seen, gender role and sexual preferences are not as clear. Gender roles based on the gender identity are learned differently from culture to culture, and from family to family. In some homes it is acceptable for men to cook and clean, and in others it is frowned upon. Sexual preference is also learned through a complex process and, while most children learn to prefer the opposite sex, some learn to prefer the same sex.

These distinctions between gender, gender identity, gender role, and sexual preference are essential. By misunderstanding them, McNeill makes a crucial error. He calls "idolatrous" the absolutizing of the separation of the sexes as male and female to reveal the image of God, thus discarding the foundational Biblical distinction between male and female as being merely biological, in order to make his case that same-sex love is part of the divine plan. However "personalist" McNeill wishes to be, and however the structure of male and female may throw into question his conclusions, he is clearly confusing gender identity and gender role. For while God has given us freedom in our choice of gender roles, He has revealed gender identity absolutes.

Thus at the basis of what it means to be human in gender identity, there is a God-ordained dualism which becomes a directive to the divine will in gender role and sexual preference. We are either male or female. Our choice is in becoming male *and* female. Will we live as heterosexual man-in-community?

Order-Freedom-Purpose

Having come thus far, we can summarize briefly. To

understand homosexuality properly we must begin with human sexuality, and we have chosen to begin with Genesis 1-3 in order to discern God's original intention for that sexuality. From this discernment we can move to understand homosexuality itself. Intrinsic in our choice to begin with Genesis is the decision to begin our search for truth with revelation—not observation; we will seek to understand what we observe in the light of what is revealed. Although there is a reciprocal relationship between revelation and observation, revelation will be given primacy.

We have defined the homosexual person as one who has a dominant erotic attraction for members of the same sex. In addition, rather than viewing gender identity, gender role, and sexual preference as static and predetermined, we have seen that those aspects of one's personality are learned. Thus we see the dynamic nature of human sexuality, yet we have also affirmed a static structure to God's revealed will for our sexuality. What more can be said about this? Where do we go from here?

Back to the Beginnings

In the opening chapters of Genesis we learn that in creation God gives us three gifts: *order, freedom,* and *purpose.* His *order* is seen in Genesis 1 as he separates light from darkness, earth from the waters, vegetation from animals according to their own kind, and man as male and female. Chaos becomes cosmos under the powerful will and word of God. Man is then placed in the garden in Genesis 2 to order his life under the command of God.

In the second chapter of Genesis we learn of man's *freedom.* Called to obey the divine will, he is also free to violate it. God wants people to love, not puppets to manipulate. Thus man is free to break the divine order and the divine law if he so chooses (Genesis 2:17). He can live against God or for God. He can live with God or away from God. Sin is not God's doing. Sin is the risk God takes in granting Man his freedom to live before Him and to live together as male and female, "naked and not ashamed" (Genesis 2:25).

Thus Man is created with order, freedom, and, finally, *purpose*. God wills that Man live as male and female to reflect His image. God wills that Man be fruitful and multiply and inhabit the earth. God wills that Man have dominion over the earth and the animals. God wills that Man keep the garden. God wills that Man live under His command in communion with Him, and, as Barth suggests, God wills for Man to share His Sabbath rest. Man is called to a partnership with God in grace. Thus, through the purpose of God given in Genesis, we learn that creation has a historical direction. It is goal oriented; it is "eschatalogical." Man is called to live before God actively pursuing His purpose in the world.

This order, freedom, and purpose of God given to man are all wrenched apart in the fall. God's order is broken: male and female now live in hiding from each other and in conflict with each other (Genesis 3:7, 16). Man exercises his freedom to become his own god, to be "like god." This freedom becomes the bondage of selfishness and isolation. Accusation characterizes the community of man and woman (Genesis 3:12).

The purpose of God is also challenged and thwarted. No longer living under the divine command, man pursues his own purpose rather than God's. Darkness has come, violence stalks the earth. Even nature itself is under the curse (Genesis 3:17). Man, his history, and his world are all stained by sin and fallen from the divine will. It is night.

Now we can begin to understand what has happened to gender identity, gender role, and sexual preference. All are God's gifts *and* God's call to us. We are to become personally what He has created us to be biologically. Here we clearly see the interrelationship of the static and dynamic dimensions of human sexuality. The static reality is seen as God's ordained design for man—heterosexual Man living in community as male and female. Here is God's gift of order to us. The dynamism of our sexuality is possible because of the freedom which God gives us. Man is free to participate in God's order or to reject it.

The divine order is still seen biologically in the duality of male and female. Yet the order is disrupted even here for a few with either indistinct genital (hermaphrodites) or two-part gender identity (transvestites).[3] Divine order is also seen in gender roles, however culturally conditioned they might be. We must live in this world concretely as male or female and not seek to escape into some bisexual, unisexual or androgynous ideal. Yet in this fallen world these roles are often binding rather than liberating and fulfilling. Under the curse they become sources of conflict and sexual stereotyping. After the fall, naked and ashamed, we cover up and become accusative.

Furthermore, in our sexual preference, the divine purpose is still seen in the blessing of male and female calling them to be fruitful and multiply. Here, again, is our calling to live in community as male and female—not male/male or female/female. But sex is now fraught with conflict and guilt. Faithfulness becomes faithlessness. Promiscuity is the order of the day. Life is "x-rated."

Application—The Biblical Witness

Applying these observations to homosexuality, we see that God gives us the gift to be male or female. The sign of that gift is our dual sexual structure. God then calls us to live as male or female. At the same time, God gives us the gift to be male and female. Again, He then calls us to live that way. This call, however, may be rejected.

Sin disrupts God's order and homosexuality bears witness to that disruption. Paul shows in Romans 1:26f that the homosexual person no longer knows that God has created him to live as male and female. Nature is thereby violated in homosexual acts.

The divine gift of freedom for man means that instinct no longer rules. We *learn* our gender identity, our gender role, and our sexual target (preference). God reveals to us His will in each case. Our sin, however, way-lays us. Gender roles become debilitating. Sexual targeting becomes confused. The result is that in our culture, one out of ten males have had extensive homosexual experience (Kinsey). The remainder of the Bible records the sorry confusion of sin's work in the world. This is seen, among other things, in the specific Biblical passages on homosexuality.

Here we must again stress our basic methodological point. It is only on the basis of human sexuality as male and female in Genesis 1-2 that we can understand the Biblical view of homosexuality. If we start our discussion of the Bible with the specific passages on homosexuality (as all gay advocates do) rather than with the opening chapters of Genesis, it is like trying to understand a tree by starting with the branches. Forgetting that the branches come from the trunk, we can dispose of them one by one without ever understanding their origin or their interrelationship. Only as the specific passages on homosexuality, like branches, are related to the trunk of Genesis, do they make a tree. Here and here alone is established their proper presupposition and context. Do what you will with the branches—connect them to the Israelite fear of pagan cultic pollution, or the reverence for the male seed, or the need for population growth, or the desire to survive death in one's children—they all make interesting floral arrangements for historical window dressing, but apart from the trunk we will never understand the tree! And it is from the trunk of human sexuality that the limbs of homosexuality grow.

Having understood Genesis 1-3, the rest of the Bible falls into place. Sodom and Gibeah become illustrations, not merely of the violation of hospitality, but of the violent challenge to God's order for human sexuality. The sin of Sodom is shocking and proverbial because God's order for man to relate sexually as male and female is attacked. The Levitical laws in the Holiness Code become laws bearing the divine order against a specific sin: male homosexual acts. These laws also presuppose the order of Genesis 1 and stand not merely in a cultic context, but in a proper theological context.

The New Testament affirms the order of creation in both Jesus' teaching and in Paul's letters. Heterosexuality is always presupposed. Thus Romans 1:26f illustrates the wrath of God and Man's confusion and sin in the loss of sexual identity. Male & female homosexual acts are against nature because they violate Man as male and female.

The vice catalogues in I Corinthians 6 and I Timothy 1 also reveal that homosexual acts are among the sins which exclude us from the Kingdom of God and thus stand under God's judgment. At this, we might entertain the objection that it is all terrible legalism. Did not Jesus come to free us from the law? Isn't the issue for us only the content of our sexual relationships as loving and fulfilling, rather than the structure in which they take place? Doesn't this fulfill the only Christian law, the law of love?

For the Bible, Jesus did not come to free us from the law but to fulfill the law (Matthew 5:17). Paul interprets our freedom from the law as freedom from its curse (Galatians 3:13), its power (Romans 7:9), and its ritual (Galatians 5:2). We are never free, however, from its moral intention. In Romans 8:4 the Apostle tells us that the "just requirement of the law [is] . . . fulfilled in us, who walk not according to the flesh but according to the Spirit." Thus the homosexual is never to be left in his homosexuality. After warning that those who engage in both passive and active homosexual behavior never inherit God's Kingdom, Paul continues and says, "And such were some of you. But you were washed, you were sanctified, you were justified in the name of the Lord Jesus Christ and in the Spirit of our God" (I Corinthians 6:11). The homosexual life-style is not to be affirmed, it is to be cleansed away.

What, then, is the just requirement of the law which is to be fulfilled in us? It is God's intention that we live according to the order, freedom and purpose which He established in creation. For our sexuality this means living together as male and female in the covenant of marriage which now reflects the relationship between Christ and His church (Ephesians 5:31-32). The New Testament rules out adultery, fornication and homosexual acts as proper expressions of sexuality. All violate God's intention that male and female be "one flesh." None display the relationship of Christ and the church. Biblical ethics are not antinomian; neither are they simply humanistic. We are not fulfilled simply in "loving relationships" without regard to their structure. If this were the only standard, what ground would there be for excluding loving, fulfilling incest or beastiality? Paul did not ask whether the man living with his father's wife had a loving relationship. He simply demanded that the man be removed (I Corinthians 5:1ff). At all points loving sexual relationships must be in accord with the divine order as male and female.

Moreover, the Bible is not indifferent to structure. It is through *form* that content is revealed. The content of Jesus' love is revealed by his taking the form of a servant (Philippians 2:5ff). The form must properly express the content. Content without regard to form is super-spiritual or gnostic, not Biblical Christianity. Through the form of Man as male and female the image of God is seen. Man stands alone before God in an I-Thou relationship and together with his neighbor in an I-Thou relationship. For the image of God to be fully seen, the neighbor of man must be woman. Furthermore, for the sexual relationship to be expressed ("be fruitful and multiply," "The two shall become one flesh") the neighbor must be that of the opposite sex. All else is demonic (Barth).

In this light then, homosexuality has its origin in the violation of God's gift of freedom by selecting the wrong sexual target. The homosexual person has lost touch with God's purpose for his or her sexuality. In homosexuality there is the return to chaos from cosmos. The same is true of fornication, adultery and all unloving, impersonal heterosexual relationships. As Barth points out, God gives woman to man and man says "Yes," not to woman, but to God in the presence of woman. As fallen men, however, we say "No" to God and "Yes" to each other in our broken sexuality. Even our "Yes" to each other is an ambivalent "Yes/No" or a "Yes" to the wrong gender.

So we must affirm boldly that homosexuality has its origins not in creation but in the fall. Nature is fallen and we are fallen and homosexuality is a sign of that fall and God's wrath (Romans 1:26f). To be sure, this does not make homosexual acts worse than any other sin. We must not cast any greater moral judgment upon homosexual desire and behavior than upon any other fallen desire. We must also clearly distinguish between the desire and the action. We concur with Thielicke that the desire is best viewed as a sickness or an abnormality, just as we view pain and suffering as abnormal, that is, not according to the perfect will of God.

Modern Research—Does It Concur?

We may now ask whether modern research into the origins of homosexuality bears out our conclusion. Since all are born with undifferentiated sexuality or both hetero-sexual and homosexual potential, why do some become heterosexual and others homosexual?

Part of the answer appears to lie in the Freudian model of ineffective parenting. Part of the answer also lies in a culture where there is strong male competition rather than cooperation. A heroic male ideal produces a high incidence of homosexuality as those who are unable to reach that ideal try to import their masculinity from other males. Also, where there is also an absence of a hetero-sexual option in early male puberty homosexuality can become a self-erotic solution. We must be careful not to over-simplify a vastly complex learning process, but the data is there. What is this but a comment on the impact of a fallen society upon fallen man? Homosexuality is an erotic compensation and solution for the failure of sinful man and his sinful world.

Because of this, it is absurd to idealize the homosexual as a "total person," a whole, fulfilled human being in contrast to heterosexual "half-persons." Two shoes when united make a pair, but one right shoe is only part of a pair and two right shoes together are only more of the same. Where the presumed values and advantages of ho-mosexuality are closely scrutinized, they begin to vanish.

For example, Clark holds that since the homosexual has learned to love himself in his totality he is now free to love another like himself. McNeill agrees with Clark that the homosexual is a "whole person," beyond the half-images of male or female. Thus he is able to love another out of his own fulness.

This proposition, however, is at best naive and at worst

propagandist. If the homosexual were entirely whole, there would be no way to explain his desire for erotic conquest. For both heterosexual and homosexual, erotic impulses arise from a need to possess the other. Tripp holds that the homosexual seeks a symbolic possession of the male attributes of another to fill out the "illusion of completeness." Theologically, Clark and McNeill confuse sexual love (eros) with self-giving love (agape). Sexual desire is always, in C. S. Lewis' phrase, "need-love rather than gift-love." One cannot also help but wonder whether there is really simply true love for the other here, or whether, as Freud supposed, there is not a strong element of loving the reflection on oneself in the other.

If the homosexual relationship were the ideal, then why, as Tripp shows, is it so hard to sustain? Promiscuity is not simply the curse of the male homosexual culture because of the false masculine conquest images. It is also supported because homosexual relationships are over-close and prone to fatigue. Partners of the same sex are just too much alike.

Rather than embodying the new cultural ideal, the sexual force of homosexual relationships, according to Tripp, lasts on an average of five to seven years for males and two to three years for females. Two likes appear to create boredom rather than fulfilment. Again, as Tripp shows, love between two equals never reaches erotic heights. God's creating Man as male and female, however, holds the necessary tension and distance.

Furthermore, McNeill proposes that the homosexual can be free from male violence and domination because he has rejected our cultural stereotypes. In this way he is free to serve others more readily and is more spiritually open because of his passive-receptive attitude. He can even bear more directly the attributes of Christ Himself in such service.

Here McNeill seems to engage in the worst kind of

sexual stereotyping of gender roles. His descriptions fit exactly the way heterosexuals commonly view homosexuals as weak, self-effacing, passive people, which is fatal to his own argument. He is even forced to reject his own stereotype later and admit that there is no real difference between heterosexuals and homosexuals.

It has also been proposed that as homosexual persons emerge out of their closets, they will bring more freedom and pluralism to our culture. This may well be true. For example, homosexuals may well free heterosexuals from our cultural stereotypes of what it means to be male or female. Our suspicion, however, is that this will happen more authentically as men and women work together to free each other from their stereotypes.

In summary, while homosexuality is deviant, much of it is created by a deviant culture, as we have seen. Culture which idealizes heroic competition and achievement is more Graeco-Roman than Biblical. As Jesus puts it, "You know that those who are supposed to rule over the Gentiles lord it over them, and their great men exercise authority over them. But it shall not be so among you; but whoever would be great among you must be your servant, and whoever would be first among you must be slave of all. For the Son of man also came not to be served but to serve, and to give His life as a ransom for many" (Mark 10:42-45). A culture where this was the male ideal would quite certainly be a culture with little or no homosexuality. Thus the culture which contributes to homosexuality contradicts New Testament values. As the church supports a worldly value system of competition, power and success, rather than cooperation and service, it shares the guilt for homosexuality. This being so, what is our message to the church?

To the Church

To begin with, the church must repent of its own homophobia. This irrational fear of homosexuals has cut gay people off from the gospel and the redemptive community it creates. While it is true that we must embody the reality of Man as male and female, it is also true that we are all sinners. In so far as we reject homosexual human beings because of our own neurotic fears of our homosexual potential, or of their being "different," we must repent.

The failure of the church to minister effectively to homosexuals has brought about such aberrations as the gay Metropolitan Community Church. This stands as a judgment upon us. Our failure has also brought gay Christians into openly demanding full endorsement for their homosexual life-styles. They want the church to say, "Gay is Good."

In the crisis of how the church is to understand homosexuality and what her ministry to homosexuals is to be, we may hear again the call of Christ to find our security not in our heterosexual identity, but in Him. Then we must turn and reach out to struggling gay Christians, and to the masses of homosexuals who lie beyond them, untouched by the gospel. What then should the church's ministry to gays be?

Having repented (or being repentant) of our homophobia, and believing in the power of the gospel, the first responsibility of the church is the same for homosexuals as for all: we must proclaim Jesus Christ and Him crucified as the resurrected Lord, and call all to faith in Him.

The first word of the gospel to a homosexual is not "stop it," "change your sexual preference," or "go into therapy." The first word of the gospel is not to *do* anything. The first word is God. He alone created us; He alone can redeem us; He alone can give us new life and the hope that it brings. Our call is not to change ourselves but to turn from our rebellion against Him and from our unbelief and place our faith solidly in Jeus Christ. It is only Christ, through the power of the Holy Spirit, who can do the changing. What a relief! What good news for gays! Your sexual condition is not a "static" reality! Christ offers you a new orientation. Come to Christ and He will do the changing.

Next the homosexual must be told that when he places his faith in Christ he belongs to the body of Christ. The issue of church membership for advocating and practicing homosexuals is an ecclesiastical issue, not a Biblical issue. We do not join the church, we are joined to the church through the work of God's Spirit as we offer ourselves to Him (Romans 12:1-5). Thus the gay person is joined to a forgiving, redemptive, loving, truthful, and yes, disciplining body of believers. It is here that he receives the hope and the power to be changed.

Available to gay Christians must be a professional program of psychological counseling to help them understand where they have come from and how the dynamics of change operate within them. This will include help in new emotional openness to the opposite sex and the reprogramming of sexual fantasies. It will also include realism about abandoning contacts in the homosexual world.

If gay Christians are properly instructed in the faith and if they are open to God's work, then they will have a new motivation to change. This then must be reinforced by the Christian community wherein change is its lifestyle, as it is growing up into Christ. Here is "gracious living," not legal performance.

In counseling homosexuals I have encountered two primary tasks. The first is to help the homosexual understand grace. God's forgiveness is free; it is also unqualified and unconditional. Many homosexuals come to Christ carrying a great load of guilt. Many will struggle with failure in their Christian lives. For them the gospel must be preached in authority and power. Christ forgives! He forgives freely! If we try to atone for our own sin, then we diminish the work of Christ.

The second task is to offer hope to the Christian homosexual. The Christian community is to be a community of hope. The church is the gifted body of Christ where speaking the truth in love causes us to grow up in Him. In that community, in the process of sanctification, God's renewed order of Man as male and female will be seen. Here healthy heterosexual role models will emerge. Here there will be warmth, openness, and the absence of threat. Here the individual will find a new family of brothers and sisters in Christ. Their word to each other is always a word of hope. Sin does not have the last word: only Christ does—and our hope is to be conformed to Him.

I am absolutely convinced that we have not begun to see what God can do through the church in bringing gay people to Himself and giving them a new sexual identity. We have not seen this because we do not welcome the witness of many homosexual Christians who, in Christ, *have* been changed in their sexual orientation to become heterosexual. This silent change has gone unnoticed and unreported.

In the context of the Christian community, then, as a homosexual's sexual preference emerges, he needs to be told the following things.

To the Homosexual

In the first place, being gay is not your identity. Behind your sexual preference and your gender role is God's revealed order for your gender identity. Like all the rest of mankind you are either male or female. You must begin there. Furthermore, your gender role and sexual preference are both learned. Therefore, they have the potential for modification or relearning. You are not stuck where you are by an unchanging human nature. You are not a "static homosexual." You are not an "invert." As you have homosexual potential, so you have heterosexual potential. This is God's gift of freedom to you, however it has been distorted.

In the second place, if you have come to Christ you have received a new identity in Him. Claim that identity! This means radical personal and moral change. We are all going through this together in our own ways as the Christian community. We are putting off the old man, we are putting on the new. This is the basis for our adventure of faith. We are in Christ and now being conformed to Him.

In the third place, gay is not good. God's will for you is to be both male *or* female and male *and* female. Thus we are to say "Yes" to God for giving us the opposite sex with which to be in community. You are to use the gift of freedom which God has given you to move into His will. That is His purpose for you. You must affirm this by faith and by your openness to God's confirmation of this in your experience.

In the fourth place, being changed in your sexual orientation is not hopeless. As Paul says, ". . . and such *were* some of you. . . ." Once the structures of invert/pervert have been abandoned, change becomes an option for you. Change is not, however, simply a matter of prayer and discipline. Your change must be nourished by a sensitive, loving, informed Christian community.

In the fifth place you may consider alternatives to change. Celibacy may be one, if God's special gift and call are received freely. The discipline of continence may be another. As abhorrent as it may seem in our sex-saturated culture, living a life without acting out our sexual desires is not inhuman. Many Christians, in obedience to God, make that free choice. All are called to live that way before marriage. There are many positive benefits from such a decision as well as the obvious negative ones. We are promised, however, that God's grace is sufficient for our needs.

Conclusions for the Church

For the church at this point to surrender to gay advocacy and gay theology and thus to give up her Biblical faith would bring not only disaster upon herself, it would bring more havoc to the world as well. If the church simply blesses homosexuality, the hope for change in Christ will be destroyed. Millions of potential converts will have the only lasting hope for wholeness cut off from them. Untold numbers of children and adolescents who are struggling with their sexual identity will conclude that "gay is good," deny their heterosexual potential and God's heterosexual purpose for them, and slip into the brokenness of the gay world. Untold numbers of adults will follow suit.

For the church herself there will be a tragic theological disaster. If the church follows the social sciences by viewing homosexual persons as "static" and as "inverts" who cannot be changed, she will be saying that God is now revealing new truth in nature which contradicts the Bible. At this point the church will become structually cultic in her theology. The Mormons and Jehovah's Witnesses all claim "new" revelation which contradicts and abuses the Bible. The Protestant Reformers all demanded that claims to new revelation be tested "according to the scriptures." The assertion that God is saying "gay is good" fails that test.

Nature, although created by God, does not reveal the unclouded will of God. There is always potential distortion. If ten percent of the male population is homosexual, that proves nothing about the will of God. Conversely, if ninety percent of the male population is heterosexual, that too *proves* nothing about the will of God. God's will is not the result of a majority vote. Jesus' death upon the cross was majority rejection, yet that changed nothing about His revelatory and redemptive work.

Furthermore, nature is both structured and variable. By what criterion shall we embrace its structure and by what criterion shall we embrace its variation? The Christian answer affirms the criterion of Scripture. Here is the sure word. In understanding human sexuality, we have found that sure word throughout the Scriptures.

What then about the ordination of avowed and practicing homosexuals into the Christian ministry? It is undoubtedly true that the church has ordained many homosexuals. They have, however, never declared their sexual preference. If a homosexual Christian seeks to enter the ministry while admitting that his or her homosexuality is a sin, and while being in a state of repentance, then there is no bar to ordination. All clergymen are repentant sinners. No sin is special before God. Such a person must then live a life of celibacy or be changed by Christ to a heterosexual orientation.

The crisis comes for the church when people who are "avowed and practicing" homosexuals desire to be ordained. A *practicing* homosexual is one who engages in homosexual behavior; an *avowed* and *practicing* homosexual not only engages in homosexual behavior, but also affirms the practice of homosexuality and admits his or her intention to continue this practice. The key word here is "avowed." (Though perhaps "self-approving" would better express our meaning here. Let us, however, continue to use "avowed," as it is common in the contemporary debate.) If the church ordains avowed and practicing homosexuals, then the church will ordain ministers who are advocates of a non-biblical understanding of man and of a life-style which is out of the will of God. Their advocacy will endorse that which is called sin in the Scriptures, that which is an "abomination" (Leviticus 18:22), that which is a sign of the wrath of God (Romans 1:26), that which stands under the judgment of God (Romans 1:27), that which receives the divine decree of death (Romans 1:32), that which excludes one from the Kingdom of God (I Corinthians 6:9), and that which is contrary to sound doctrine (I Timothy 1:10). Shall we fill our pulpits with such advocates? Shall we make such advocates pastors of our people? Shall the Word of God be proclaimed and taught by such advocates?

Moreover, we find that the question of whether or not avowed and practicing homosexuals should be ordained is a specific instance of a more general question: Should the church ordain a person who admits his intention to commit actions which the Bible judges as sinful? It seems clear that the answer to this question is "No." Even those who defend the ordination of homosexual persons do not deny this response. They do, however, deny that homosexual behavior is sinful.

The avowed and practicing homosexual who seeks ordination admits his or her intention to engage in homosexual behavior after being ordained. If the church believes that the Bible judges homosexual behavior to be sinful, then homosexual Christians should not be ordained.

We have seen the complete Biblical treatment of homosexuality. We have seen that homosexual actions are indeed sinful. About this there can be little doubt. Therefore we stand firm in our position that avowed and practicing homosexual persons should not be ordained to Christian ministry. To sweeten sin by calling attention to the love and sincerity of advocating and practicing homosexual Christians is to miss the point. Many times I have been a loving and sincere sinner. At the point of my sin, however, I am called not to rationalize but to repent. If sin is destructive to me, if it is a lethal poison, then the most loving word is not "drink more," but "stop it."

In dealing with homosexual Christians, we must be careful to examine ourselves. Are we conscious of our own sin? Are we broken before the cross? Do we come to erring brothers and sisters, not to judge or condemn, but to heal and to save? Are we willing to bear their burdens with them? Will we restore them in a "spirit of gentleness" and so fulfill the law of Christ which is the law of love (Galatians 6: 1-2)?

There is a balance between truth and love which is hard to achieve. The truth must be spoken about homosexuality. We must not flinch or back away here. As Luther says, "If I profess with the loudest voice and clearest exposition every portion of the truth of God except precisely that little point which the world and the Devil are at that moment attacking, I am not confessing Christ, however boldly I may be professing Christ. Where the battle rages, there the loyalty of the soldier is proved, and to be steady on all the battlefield besides, is mere flight and disgrace if he flinches at that point."

At the same time, the truth must be spoken in love (Ephesians 4:15). The homosexual person is made in the image of God. He or she is loved by Christ, called by Christ, forgiven by Christ, offered a new life by Christ, and welcomed into the church by Christ. Here Jesus makes all things new. Homosexual Christians will help to deliver us from our homophobia as we begin to see them as people. Homosexual Christians will become witnesses to the power of Christ as He changes their sexual orientation. Homosexual Christians will help to deliver us from our sexual stereotypes and homosexual Christians will help us to open doors for Christ's truth and grace to penetrate the gay world.

This is a moment of unequalled opportunity and peril for the church. Our opportunity lies in redeeming a rejected and despised minority. Our opportunity lies in bringing the changing power of Christ to them. Our peril lies in sacrificing the truth of God's Word, the integrity of the church and the intentions of God in creating us male and female, on the altar of relativism and modernity.

Such a sacrifice would be a theological, ecclesiastical and social catastrophe. The church would become cultic, embracing a new anti-biblical "revelation." Denominations would be split and abandoned by millions of faithful Christians. Society would be rushed down the path of disintegration and countless young lives would be left in sexual chaos and ruin. Rather than these little ones being offended, it would be better for a millstone to be placed around our necks and for us to be cast into the sea.

Now is a time for truth. Now is a time for love. In the crisis God promises His miracle. He alone brings life out of death. May we in faith see that life: new life for the church and new life for millions of lonely, guilty, struggling people who in actualizing their homosexual potential have missed God's order, violated God's freedom, and lost God's purpose for them. His purpose for us is that we live as male *or* female and male *and* female, reflecting the image of God in the world together as that image is made new in Christ.

Appendix

A Critical Review of the Task Force Report on Homosexuality of the United Presbyterian Church in the U.S.A.

Responding to requests from two Presbyteries in 1976, the General Assembly of the United Presbyterian Church commissioned a task force to study the ordination of avowed and practicing homosexual persons. The 190th General Assembly will act upon that study when it meets in May, 1978 at San Diego, California.

This review of the task force's report comes from the "inside." Having served as one of its nineteen members for a year and a half, I have shared the laborious study process which has resulted in a Background Paper written by Byron Shaffer, Professor of Old Testament at Fordham University in New York. Working from Shaffer's original draft, the task force debated many sections of the report and resolved their disagreements by majority vote. Since the minority were theologically conservative (5 of 19), they were often outvoted in the content decisions.

The Background Paper is followed by a policy statement and recommendations from the majority and the minority. The majority of the task force favors the ordination of avowed and practicing homosexual persons while the minority opposes such action.

Our review will focus on an analysis of the Background Paper which provides the platform upon which the recommendations of the majority and minority stand.

The Background Paper, a book in itself, covers four major sections: *I. Homosexuality: Psychotherapy and the Empirical Sciences; II. Homosexuality and the Bible: a re-examination; III. The Church's Ministry to/with/ among/for homosexual persons; IV. Homosexuality and Ordination in the United Presbyterian Church*. The Biblical section examines the Old and New Testament texts which mention some form of homosexuality. Then four theological models, from conservative to liberal, expose divergent approaches to the Bible and apply their presuppositions and principles to the understanding of homosexuality. While the Background Paper employs careful "scientific" scholarship, it moves from a particular point of view which determines the selection of data and prepares for the majority outcome favoring the ordination of homosexual persons. We will return to this point later. Let us now examine the document itself.

In the first major section, *Homosexuality: Psychotherapy and the Empirical Sciences*, attention is given to biology, psychology, and sociology. Each discipline is explored as it relates to the development of gender, gender identity and role, and sexual preference in the homosexual person. The spirit and style of this section is descriptive rather than evaluative; no theological "intrusion" is allowed. At the same time, a bias rapidly emerges in the way the descriptive material is used. This is seen especially in the refusal to discuss the various views of the origins of homosexuality and in the ordering of the discussion on how a homosexual person develops—from the "deviant" viewpoint to the "variant" viewpoint to the "normal" viewpoint. The concluding "normal" viewpoint is the one which stays with the reader.

In this section, alternative definitions of homosexuality are noted (no page numbers will be offered because the document is in manuscript form and not yet in print at the time when this is written). The most common definition views homosexuality as an affectional orientation rather than a pattern of overt behavior. If one experiences a dominant erotic attraction to the same sex one is homosexual. Few, however, are exclusively homosexual. Here Kinsey's research is offered as documentation. Thus, "homosexual" and "heterosexual" are not necessarily exclusive categories. The Background Paper seems to endorse a "dynamic" definition of homosexuality.

While infants are biologically male or female at birth (or are surgically repaired to be so if their genital structure is indistinct), their gender identity and roles are learned. Increasingly, scientists are accepting the hypothesis that humans possess bisexual potential and gender identity comes primarily from psychosocial factors (parents, society, etc.). Thus the Task Force Report states that "one's sexual orientation is not fixed at birth. Humans are neither heterosexual nor homosexual by biological determination alone." While gender identity, gender role, and sexual preference are learned, this does not mean that the child is conscious of the factors shaping his or her sexual identity.

It is at this point that the background paper makes a crucial turn. Because there is no consensus on what psychosocial factors are determinitive in shaping sexual identity, a review of the specific causes of homosexuality is rejected. This is decisive. If I am ignorant of the origin of something, then I am limited in my ability to evaluate it. I may be able to judge its results, but an understanding of its essence will elude me. For example, the worship of pagan gods may have beneficial social results for a society and even valuable psychological results for the devotees. But I can understand idolatry as sin only when I know that I am created to worship the one, true God. Likewise, homosexuality is a deviation from God's will because we are created to be male and female and to express our erotic desire heterosexually.

In contrast to the task force, our own analysis of homosexuality leads us to conclude that it largely comes from inadequate family structure, the absence of opposite sex targets in early puberty, and idealized cultural identity models which create the need to import more of the same-sex erotically into oneself. Thus, theologically, homosexuality originates from fallen human nature living in a fallen world. In Tripp's words, it comes from the need to possess another like oneself, and thereby to fulfill the illusion of completeness.

Three approaches to the development of homosexuality are noted by the Background Paper. It may be a deviant development, a variant development or a normal development.

The deviant development theory is rejected by the Background Paper for two reasons. Because we are born with bisexual potential, heterosexuality cannot be established as an inborn tendency, thus making homosexuality deviant. Furthermore, the attempts to change homosexual persons to heterosexuality have not met with great success (that this is disputed is minimized by the Background Paper).

The variant development theory sees homosexuality as pathological only if there is evidence of destructive feelings or behavior. Thus homosexual orientation alone is not pathological; there must be other factors operating.

The normal development theory assumes that all are born bisexual and that those infants who are positively conditioned by homosexual stimuli will mature as healthy in an accepting society. In conclusion, the Background Paper accepts "multiple homosexualities" arising from nature (biology) and nurture (psychology, sociology). Some develop "as pathologies; some as successful adjustments to difficult or simply variant circumstances or psychodynamic factors; some as positive responses to reinforcing stimuli; some as successful adjustments or positive responses which subsequently turn neurotic in the face of a hostile society; some as pathologies which subsequently lose their pathological motivation and become nonpathological." As noted above, all of this is presented nontheologically in the antiseptic style of scientific description. Nurture and nature appear valueless: they are not really treated so, however, as "personal health" is seen to be the goal for a homosexual person. If a homosexual person is psychologically "healthy" in an accepting society, then, it seems assumed, this is the optimum. No question of God's order or will is allowed to intrude.

Society now becomes the villain in its fear and repression of homosexual persons through its "homophobia." It is assumed that society has created the promiscuous homosexual male by relegating his behavior to "underground" gay bars and baths. Here a naive view of male sexuality seems to be endorsed. Male promiscuity is not just carried on in the darkness. To blame society for promiscuity is psychologically and morally shallow. While it is clear that society has feared homosexual persons and repressed them, it is certain that society alone is not the cause of their pain. Society is fallen, true, but so is human nature. We are not as God intended us to be.

In summary, the strength of the section on *Homosexuality: Psychotherapy and the Empirical Sciences* is its current, careful evaluation of *one line* of evidence and discussion about homosexuality. Its weaknesses, however, are the absence of any comprehensive discussion of the origins of homosexuality, its tacit assumption that most homosexual persons cannot find a re-orientation to a heterosexual life, and its failure to evaluate the scientific data theologically. This creates the illusion of a scientific and scholarly objectivity, when, in fact, a particular argument is being pursued by a selective presentation of materials and by silence on origins. If we do not know where "homosexualities" have come from, and if we cannot assume a heterosexual ideal or norm, if we are all "bisexual," if most homosexual persons cannot be changed to heterosexuality, and if society distorts the free development of our sexual identity, then the foundation is clearly laid "scientifically" for conclusions which would view homosexuality as one natural alternative for our sexual potential. Its violation by attempts at change would, in many cases, be a violation of nature itself, or even the will of God. Is it to be doubted that this becomes the majority conclusion for the task force? As in John McNeill (*The Church and the Homosexual*), when one track of scientific study has the first word it will be likely to have the last word. Here, in Helmut Thielicke's analysis is "Cartesian theology," starting with man, not with God. Our presuppositions about homosexuality will determine our conclusions about homosexuality. We turn now to the second part of the Background Paper: *Homosexuality and the Bible; a Re-examination.*

The rise of the gay liberation movement has caused the church to re-evaluate its traditional opposition to homosexuality. This necessarily takes us back to the Bible, especially since the General Assembly of the United Presbyterian Church affirmed that "there is always more light to break forth from the Bible through the work of the Holy Spirit." What then does the Bible teach on the subject?

Here, as in the discussion of homosexual origins, a basic and determinative decision must be made. Shall we start our study with Genesis 19, the account of Sodom and Gomorrah, or shall we start with Genesis 1-3, the account of creation and the Fall?

The argument against starting with Genesis 1-3 is that homosexuality is nowhere mentioned here. The argument *for* starting with Genesis 1-3 is that the presuppositions for human sexuality are established here and that homosexuality cannot be understood apart from these presuppositions.

The Background Paper of the task force makes the unfortunate decision only to study the Biblical texts where some homosexual act is mentioned. This has the effect of trying to understand a tree by starting with its branches and overlooking its roots and trunk. Where did the branches come from? Apart from Genesis 1-3, where mankind is created according to the divine order as male and female, there is no answer. The results of this choice are clear.

The first texts considered by the Background Paper are the accounts of Sodom and Gomorrah (Genesis 18-19) and Gibeah (Judges 19-21). In each case visitors to the cities are assaulted by the natives and threatened with violent rape. In each case this rape is homosexual in its intent.

In the account of Sodom, it is admitted by the Background Paper that the violent rape was in violation of the "basic male gender schema." What is not admitted, however, is that the violent rape also violated God's order of creation where He made mankind male and female and blessed their sexual union, "Be fruitful and multiply . . ." (Genesis 1:28); "Therefore a man leaves his father and his mother and cleaves to his wife and they become one flesh . . ." (Genesis 2:24). Thus the horrendous nature of the crimes at Sodom and Gibeah are weakened. Also the sexual misconduct of Sodom and Gomorrah mentioned in II Peter 2:7 and the fornication (any sexual immorality) mentioned in Jude 7 are denied their proper basis in the violation of God's order: mankind created as male and female.

While the Background Paper asserts that in Genesis 18-19 and Judges 19-21 rape violates God's justice, it questions whether one can "discern the attitude of God toward homosexual relationships between consenting adults." We answer that indeed God's attitude can be discerned. The events at Sodom and Gibeah clearly violate God's creating us male and female to be united heterosexually as "one flesh." This understanding, as the Background Paper notes, is confirmed by II Peter 2:6-10 and Jude 7.

Next, after properly translating *qādes* as "male cult prostitute" in Deuteronomy 23:17-18, the Background Paper examines the Levitical Laws against male homosexual acts in Leviticus 18 and 20. The judgment that such acts are an "abomination'" and worthy of death is properly grounded in the "orders of creation," mankind as male and female. This unfortunately does not cause a reconsideration of the decision not to begin the Biblical section with Genesis 1-3. Since the Levitical laws against homosexuality are grounded in creation, we must consider homosexuality in relation to human sexuality (Genesis 1-3). This, however, the Background Paper refuses to do.

Moreover, the attempt to relativize those laws is made when the rhetorical question is posed unanswered, "What do Christians do with Old Testament law and with Israelite orders of creation in the light of both Jesus Christ and expanding empirical knowledge?" We reply that Jesus Christ reaffirmed the orders of creation when He appealed from the Mosaic divorce law back to the creation of male and female to become "one flesh" (Matthew 19:8), and that "expanding empirical knowledge" must always be submitted to revelation. Also, rather than having "empirical knowledge," what we actually have is a significant amount of data demanding an interpretation which will never be simply "empirical."

Turning to the New Testament, the Background Paper examines Romans 1:26-27. Here Paul sees homosexual acts for both males and females as contrary to nature (God's order in creation) and as a sign of the Divine Wrath. Rather than an exposition of these verses, however, major attention is only given to their context. Thus the importance of Romans 1:26-27 is downplayed.

Next, the Background Paper examines I Corinthians 5-6. Here in a vice-catalogue, Paul warns that homosexual persons will not inherit the kingdom of God (6:10). The translation of the words historically rendered "effeminate" (*catamite*) and "homosexual pervert" have been challenged by John Boswell. Since the challenge (unpublished) has not been reviewed by scholars and since there are clear reasons to reject it, the Background Paper properly notes that on the basis of Romans 1:26f. Paul would have included homosexual acts in his comprehensive list of pagan vices. This also applies to the similar vice-catalogue in I Timothy 1:9-10.

By its failure to see the accounts of Sodom and Gibeah in light of the orders of creation in Genesis 1-3, and by the caution before Boswell's challenge of I Corinthians 6 and I Timothy 1, the Background Paper concludes that the church must deal particularly with "the Levitical law codes and with the Apostle Paul (in Romans)." Thus, the Biblical texts have been reduced to occasional references and are not seen in the comprehensive understanding of human sexuality based upon the orders of creation. This then leads to a relativizing of these texts by the claim that Christians are free from the Levitical laws (after all we do eat pork!), and that for Paul, holiness is now fulfilled in the law of love, rather than in submitting to the orders of creation.

The relativizing of the Biblical revelation is also accomplished, in part, by a barrage of questions that stand un-answered. We will reproduce them here and attempt to answer each one as posed.

(1). *Question*: Paul and Leviticus are far removed from us in time and culture; what authority do they then have in evaluating the psychosocial phenomenon of homosexual-*ities*, the complexity of which is just now gaining empirical definition?

Answer: God has not changed, human nature has not changed, and the Holy Spirit who inspired the Biblical authors still illumines us today. Moreover, homosexual*ities* are a myth. While there are various social and psychological causes for a homosexual condition, theologically all spring from a fallen humanity and a fallen society. All are a violation of God's creation of mankind as male and female.

(2). *Question*: The ancient Israelites understood hetero-sexual marriage to be God's only created order for human sexuality. . . . Contemporary social scientists understand humans to be born *without* a pre-determined sexual orien-tation. Are the ancient view and the modern view compati-ble?

Answer: Yes, they are. God ordered human sexual-ity as male and female, yet he granted mankind the free-dom to violate that order. Thus we are free to deny our maleness or femaleness and seek same-sex erotic rela-tionships. Creation as male and female is no more deter-mined than God's command not to eat of the tree of the knowledge of good and evil (Genesis 2:17). This is the divine intention. We are free to deny it and suffer the consequences. That we have exercised that freedom which has created sexual conflict (Genesis 3:16) and homo-sexual perversion (Romans 1:26-27) is clear.

(3). *Question*: The author of Job emphasized that the mysteries of God's activities as Creator cannot be completely comprehended by the human mind (chs. 38-41). No doctrine of creation can *fully* state the truth about the Creator. Nevertheless, is it not the case that the church's knowledge of God's work as Creator continues to grow as time and experience lead to new glimpses of the Creator's plan?

Answer: Certainly the affirmation is true that as we grow in our knowledge of creation we grow in our appreciation of the Creator. Does this, however, invalidate God's creation of mankind as male and female? Shall we appeal to our scientific theories to invalidate Biblical revelation? It is one thing to "grow" in our knowledge of God as Creator and another to use our understanding of creation to contradict the Biblical understanding of the Creator. Will we now appeal to "natural revelation" to contradict scriptural revelation? Since scientific theory is constantly changing and since the scientific observer shares human relativity, dare we absolutize such theory and observers as a new word from God? Is it not also true that according to the Bible nature is corrupted by sin? Can we therefore appeal from sinful, fallen nature to a true knowledge of God? Such a project rests on a fallacious assumption and is therefore invalid.

(4). *Question*: Homosexual behavior violated the Israelite's male gender schema. Treating one's wife as an equal violated their male gender schema. Remaining single violated their male gender schema. By what criteria does the Christian decide that one part of the Israelites' male gender schema reflects God's eternal plan itself and the others only a time-conditioned human understanding of God's plan?

Answer: What is at stake in homosexual behavior is not the violation of gender schema, but the order of creation. This has already been established in the exegesis of the Background Paper itself. It is on the basis of Genesis

1-3 that homosexual behavior is rejected, not simply on the basis of a culturally relative gender schema.

(5). *Question*: Homosexual behavior between consenting males and heterosexual intercourse with a menstruating wife were both capital crimes in ancient Judah. Both violated the Israelites' understanding of holiness. By what criteria does the Christian decide that one law reflects God's eternal will itself and the other only a time-conditioned human understanding of God's will?

Answer: The judgment that the law against intercourse with a menstruating wife is a "time-conditioned human understanding of God's will" is a humanistic, secularizing judgment. That this law is time-conditioned is clear because it teaches a holiness for human life which, lacking a ground in creation, is ordered after the fall and fulfilled in Christ who completes and ends the demand of the law. This is to be clearly distinguished from the law against homosexual behavior which finds its ground in the order of creation as male and female. This order is reaffirmed by Jesus Himself (Matthew 19:4). However, He says nothing about a menstruating wife. Thus both Creation and Christ are the ground for the Biblical opposition to homosexual acts.

(6). *Question*: Paul believed that the Mosaic law had become a weapon in the arsenal of sin (Romans 7). How then can the Mosaic law be a sure guide to God's will for the Christian life?

Answer: The law is a weapon in the arsenal of sin, not because the law has failed, but because we have failed. When sin is forgiven and we are illumined by the Holy Spirit, the "just requirement of the law (is) . . . fulfilled in us who walk not according to the flesh but according to the Spirit" (Romans 8:4). God's will for the Christian life never violates this moral character revealed in the law.

(7). *Question*: Does Paul in Romans 1:18-22 quote *with approval* a traditional Jewish understanding that the Gentiles' exchange of heterosexual behavior for homosexual behavior is sin? Or does he rather cite traditional Jewish teaching about Gentile sin so that when his Jewish Christian readers nod assent to such self-satisfied, judgmental rhetoric he may then forcefully remind them of their sole dependence upon faith for justification before God?

Answer: If Paul does not quote the traditional argument against homosexual behavior *with approval*, then his conclusion collapses. How could his Jewish Christian readers be convicted if the arguments leading to that conviction are fallacious?

(8). *Question*: In either case, there can be no doubt that Paul understood the *self-satisfied* condemnation of the other person's sin to be itself sin. Are expressions of anti-homosexual attitudes by some Christians examples of such sin?

Answer: We can suspect that some Christians have a self-satisfied attitude in their condemnation of homosexual persons. This attitude is a sin. Does the sin of self-satisfaction, however, cancel the sin of homosexuality?

(9). *Question*: Let us assume that Paul did accept the Jewish view that pagans, out of unfit minds and consciences, had consciously chosen to replace heterosexual behavior with homosexual behavior. Today, most homosexual persons have made no such conscious choice. Does Romans 1:26-28 speak authoritatively of these people?

Answer: In Romans 1 Paul is not centering on conscious or unconscious choice in our sin. He does affirm that God has made His will known, so we are without excuse. He also affirms that we have rebelled against that will and surrendered the true knowledge of God. The results of this now, however, are darkness, idolatry, and immorality. Nowhere does Paul claim to offer an existential analysis of individual conscious sin. Everywhere Paul traces the fall and degradation of humankind which leads to the chaos of "a base mind and ... improper conduct" (1:28). Sunk now in our sin we all manifest the wrath of God as the infection of our evil spreads. To assume that Paul held that we all have a "conscious" choice to reenact Adam's fall is unpauline and unbiblical (compare Romans 5:15-21).

God's order is not designed now to aid our "conscious choice," but to reveal our sinful rebellion and convict us of our sin. The person who makes no conscious choice to be a homosexual is justly judged by God who has established heterosexuality as His purpose for us. An "unconscious" idolater is still an idolater and God's wrath stands against him for his violation. Fallen human nature in a fallen world is judged by God whether we are conscious or unconscious in our sin. If I break the speed limit I am a law-breaker whether or not I am willful in my act. To argue that God only judges "conscious" sin is to relativize His holiness and assert a human freedom unknown to the Bible. We are all now in the darkness and there we are all under God's righteous judgment. This then prepares us for the gospel of His grace.

(10). *Question*: Let us assume that Paul did accept the Jewish view that the pagan's homosexual behavior was always motivated by shameful, self-serving passion. Paul also believed that pagans' heterosexual marriages were motivated by self-serving passion. Just how *polemic* was Paul being? Was *all* pagan sexuality really motivated by lust? Is all homosexuality today, including that which is found among Christians, motivated by lust?

Answer: For Paul, since the end of human life is the love and service of God, all virtue directed to other ends becomes "self-serving passion." Our sexuality is only glorifying God when it is forgiven and renewed by the Holy Spirit. Only by God's *agape*, His self-giving love, can sexual love be restored to its divine purpose.

Now it is employed in the service of the other. No homosexual love can be so employed, because if a homosexual Christian loves another with Christ's love it would lead to the cessation of violating God's intention that human sexuality be expressed heterosexually. The love of another must be according to the will of God. If it is contrary to the will of God it is not love.

(11). *Question*: Paul understood this created world to be in bondage and decay. Therefore he did not believe that the "form of this world," including the pattern of heterosexual marriage, could be regarded as an unquestioned guide for the Christian life. Paul's guide for the Christian life was "the new creation," which is "faith working through love." Such faith working through love can transform a self-serving married heterosexuality (part of the old creation) into an honoring, self-giving, married heterosexuality (part of the new creation). Is it possible that faith working through love can transform a self-serving homosexuality (part of the old creation) into an honoring, self-giving homosexuality (part of the new creation)?

Answer: The confusion here is in viewing heterosexual marriage as simply the "form of this world," a part of the old creation. Heterosexual marriage is a part of God's order of creation *before the fall*. Thus the gospel does not deny it, but redeems it. To ask for the redemption of homosexuality, however, is to ask for redemption, not of God's order of creation, but of the violation of that order. Faith working through love cannot purify homosexuality any more than it can purify incest or prostitution. An honoring, self-giving incestuous relationship is still sinful since it violates God's order for human sexuality.

(12). *Question*: Paul saw a loving, faithful, permanent heterosexual marriage as the Christian's alternative to sexual immorality. Is it possible for us today . . . to see a loving, faithful, permanent homosexual relationship as the homosexual Christian's alternative to sexual immorality?

Answer: Heterosexual marriage is not simply God's answer to sin, it is God's intention for the continuation of the race and the fulfillment of man and woman as "one flesh." Here they mirror the relationship between Christ and the church (Ephesians 5:31-32). A homosexual "marriage" could be an answer to promiscuity but not to sin, since it violates God's order in creation and His fulfillment of marriage in the reflection of Christ's relationship to the church.

(13). *Question*: Paul catalogued the fruit of the Spirit —that is, the marks of sanctification: It is love, joy, peace, patience, kindness, goodness, faithfulness, gentleness, and self-control. Paul classified homosexual behavior as *porneia* (sexual immorality), a work of the flesh—that is, as a mark of sin. Today, how should the Christian community evaluate the life of a Christian who radiates love, joy, peace, patience, kindness, goodness, gentleness, and self-control and is homosexual?

Answer: Such a person is a Christian with some fruit (with the possible exception of self-control), but he or she violates the will of God in the area of human sexuality and in this respect does *not* manifest the fruit of the Spirit. In such a person, we can assume, the Spirit is at work to convict of sin in the area of sexual desire and behavior.

(14). *Question*: In matters of the freedom of Christian conscience, Paul urged Christians not to judge each other. . . . Now Paul did *not* consider homosexual behavior to be a matter of Christian conscience. He believed all immoral sexual behavior to be motivated by lust and destructive to the body. However, does the situation change if Christians discover that some homosexual behavior is motivated by love, joy, peace, patience, kindness, goodness, faithfulness, gentleness, and self-control? May such homosexual behavior be considered a matter of the freedom of Christian conscience, for which the individual should be accountable only to God?

Answer: The motivation of homosexual behavior can never be ultimately discerned by us. It probably cannot be ultimately discerned by the homosexual person either. All sexual behavior, however, has a selfish motive (eros) and therefore cannot be idealized as simply coming from "love, joy, peace, patience, kindness, etc." It is not simply the motive, however, that we are to judge, it is the behavior. Homosexual acts violate God's creation of mankind as male and female. Therefore they stem, not from "the freedom of Christian conscience," but from sin.

(15). Question: For Paul, the Jewish gender schema of male dominance over females had no salvation significance. . . . For Paul, the cultural difference between Jew and Gentile had no salvation significance. . . . For Paul, the class difference between slave and free had no salvation significance. . . . Although these particular earthly distinctions (gender, nation, class) have no salvation significance does the Christian still maintain that the earthly distinction between one sexual orientation and another does have salvation significance? Paul counseled women, Greeks, and slaves to receive sanctification within their given estates. If Paul were to understand that many homosexualities in our society are given estates, would he counsel those particular persons to receive sanctification outside their given estate rather than within it?

Answer: Since Paul saw homosexual relations as

a violation of God's estate of mankind created as male and female, he could never advocate the sanctification of a homosexual relationship. For Paul, what is necessary for the homosexual person is repentance and transformation. As he writes to the Corinthians, homosexual perverts will never inherit the Kingdom of God—but "you were washed, you were sanctified, you were justified in the name of the Lord Jesus Christ and in the Spirit of our God" (I Corinthians 6:11). An estate which is morally neutral in its origin can be sanctified. An estate which violates God's will must be changed.

(16). *Question*: The Pastoral Epistles emphasize that the key to sanctification is correct teaching enthusiastically received:

> I Tim. 2:9-15 (RSV): . . . women should adorn themselves modestly and sensibly in seemly apparel, not with braided hair or gold or pearls or costly attire but by good deeds, as befits women who profess religion. Let a woman learn in silence with all submissiveness. I permit no woman to teach or to have authority over men; she is to keep silent. For Adam was formed first, then Eve; and Adam was not deceived, but the woman was deceived and became a transgressor. Yet woman will be saved through bearing children, if °they continue° in faith and love and holiness with modesty (° . . . ° reading with the Greek text as per RSV footnote).

Does the United Presbyterian Church really believe that this passage from I Timothy is correct teaching to which the sanctifying Spirit conforms the ordinary Christian woman? If the church through the dynamic Spirit has been led to a new understanding of what it means in the sight of the Creator God to be male and female, is it not conceivable that the church is being led by the dynamic Spirit to a new understanding of what it means in the sight of the Creator God to be heterosexual and homosexual?

Answer: The heart of the question about I Timothy

2:9-15 is whether we have correct teaching here for the ordinary Christian woman. Who could argue that a Christian woman should adorn herself in a manner consistent with her faith? Not flashy dress but good deeds are to demonstrate her character.

Whether Paul goes on to prohibit women from ever teaching or having authority over men is disputed. The verb tense is present active indicative and may be translated, "I am not presently permitting a woman to teach or to have authority over men. . . ." This is necessary because of the abuse of teaching by newly liberated women in Ephesus as reflected in I Timothy. Furthermore, although Eve was deceived first, women are now the human means of salvation since, "woman will be saved through bearing children" (literally, "through bearing the child" = the Messiah). Thus while the first woman was deceived, womankind becomes the means of Christ's entrance into the world.

Salvation, however, is not simply automatic. Women must have faith, love, and live holy lives. We conclude that the United Presbyterian Church is fully justified in believing that this passage is correct teaching for the ordinary Christian woman. Thus it provides no analogy for a new understanding of homosexuality by the church.

(17). *Question*: In the absence of a direct word from the Lord to illuminate a given ethical situation, Paul felt free to offer his own ethical counsel, informed as he believed it to be, by the Spirit. In the absence of any direct word of Jesus in the Gospels on the matter of homosexuality, is the church not free to offer its own ethical counsel, informed, as it hopes it to be, by the Spirit?

Answer: While Jesus offers no direct word on homosexuality, He does offer a direct word on heterosexuality. God created us as male and female to become one flesh, "from the beginning" (Matthew 19:4). Since homosexuality must be understood from human sexuality, the church is not free to offer ethical counsel which violates Jesus' understanding of creation and the clear scriptural teaching that homosexuality is sin.

At this point we can conclude that although all of these questions are serious, they can be directly answered. The Biblical revelation cannot be relativized by such objections to the fundamental reality: Man is created male and female.

Following these questions the Background Paper turns to alternative positions on Biblical authority. Four are presented representing a spectrum of theology from conservative to liberal. Here we are confronted by the pluralism of the church.

Model A is designed to represent a strict orthodox position. Model B retains a "high" view of Scripture but is more open to cultural complexity. Model C refuses to absolutize the Scriptures, opting for a dialectic between the Spirit in Scripture and the Spirit-within-the-contemporary-church. Model D sees all of life as a process in response to God as active love, this is the only norm. The minority of the task force is best represented by model B. The majority is best represented by model C. Thus the majority finds itself free to disregard even Leviticus and Paul in calling for the ordination of avowed and practicing homosexual persons.

The position of model C is clearly stated, "Thus, the primary ethical issue in relationships between Christians is not whether the relationship conforms to a concept of 'orders of creation' but whether for the persons involved the relationship encourages and sustains growth in faith and self-giving love." In other words, the structure of the relationship is irrelevant, as long as the content "encourages and sustains growth in faith and self-giving love." By inference, an incestuous or polygamous relationship is moral as long as it is growing in faith and self-giving love.

Does God care so little for form? Can form be so easily separated from content? Is not the meaning of life or the quality of life expressed in the form of life? Is not "growing in faith and self-giving love" easily reduced to mere humanism? Is there not something essential about the form of male and female bound in a monogamous union which cannot be duplicated in any other form?

Both the Bible and contemporary medical research seem to answer this final question in the affirmative. As Tripp shows, a male/male or female/female relationship usually lacks the sexual tension necessary to sustain it.

Furthermore, for the Bible, true content is always seen through true form. We cannot claim to follow Jesus and live a style of life that contradicts that claim. We cannot claim to be fully human and not live as male *or* female and as male *and* female without contradicting God's intention in creating us.

Model C notes that while we have been created to walk we have been given the freedom to learn to fly. By analogy, although we have been created as heterosexuals we are free to become homosexuals. Is this a proper analogy, however? We assert not. Nowhere in the Bible is there a moral condemnation of flying. Flying is morally neutral. We can only judge the morality of flying by its outcome. In the Bible, however, there is a clear condemnation of homosexuality. Thus homosexuality is not morally neutral; it is a deviation from God's heterosexual intention for us in creation.

Model C employs another analogy in justifying the acceptance of avowed and practicing homosexual persons. In New Testament times, the Jews despised and excluded Gentiles. Peter, however, was called to Cornelius, a

God-fearing Gentile. Through him Peter learned that God had cleansed and sanctified the Gentiles within their Gentile estate—God had done a new thing. The same reality, it is argued, is now seen among some homosexual Christians.

While it is true that God sanctified and saved the Gentiles, much to the surprise of narrow-minded Jews, there is no Biblical condemnation of Gentiles as such similar to the Biblical condemnation of homosexuality. To the contrary, Gentiles are all created by God and are the objects of His grace. Jesus commissions His disciples to go to all the Gentile nations (Matthew 28:18-20).

Furthermore, in so far as Gentiles represent idolatrous, pagan life, they are not sanctified as pagans. They are called to a new life, to turn from their sin and to embrace the God of Israel. God's "new thing" is not to sanctify idolatrous Gentiles or even God-fearing Gentiles (such as Cornelius), but to change them. Thus God does not sanctify homosexual persons by leaving them as homosexuals, but by changing them and by calling them to His heterosexual order for all mankind.

To appeal to homosexual "Corneliuses" is to miss the point. Cornelius was not immoral as a Gentile. A homosexual person is immoral as a practicing homosexual. Cornelius was called out of his old sinful life to Christ. A homosexual person is likewise called out of his or her old sinful life to Christ. It is impossible to sanctify the estate of homosexuality because the estate as such is contrary to God's order and a sign of His wrath (Romans 1:26f.).

The standard for new life in Christ is not a subjective apprehension of the "maturing faith and self-giving love" of a homosexual person without regard for the will of God as He orders life. The Holy Spirit never sanctifies us in our sin. He calls us out of our sin, cleansing us from our sin. The Holy Spirit never works today in contradiction to the Scriptures.

When Model C claims that although the Bible speaks negatively of homosexual behavior, it also speaks about "the mysteriousness of (the Spirit's)... movement and about the unmistakable effectiveness of its action," in order to justify the sanctification of homosexuality today, Model C sets the Word against the Spirit. At this point it becomes cultic. The Biblical norm for judging claims to new revelation is lost. We have become enthusiasts and are in the same position as Mormons and Jehovah's Witnesses who claim new revelations which go beyond the Scriptures. With this, Model C dives into pure subjectivity. Revelation is now in nature and experience, rather than in the Bible seen in the light of Jesus Christ, the Word become flesh.

Following the analysis of medical and Biblical data on homosexuality, the Background Paper turns in part III to models for ministry among homosexual persons.

This section begins with a treatment of homophobia in the church, that is, the fear of homosexuals. The results of a survey made among United Presbyterians leads to the conclusion that most people in the church understand homosexuality apart from any contact with homosexual persons. Such aloofness is due to the fear of one's own homosexual urges, the threat homosexuality poses to one's own gender identity (how males or females should act), jealousy toward homosexual persons who are free from the restrictions of marriage, and the threat that homosexual persons pose to those who need children as a psychic guarantee of their immortality. The church is called to repent of such homophobia.

Two models for ministry are then proposed. The first assumes that homosexual behavior *per se* is sin. This model calls for homosexual Christians to renounce their "active homosexual lifestyle and find fulfillment either in celibacy or in a responsible heterosexual lifestyle." To accomplish this the church must call homosexual persons to repent, offer a counseling ministry oriented toward change, use the sacraments to this end, and engage in positive teaching on human sexuality. Positive role models need to be offered for heterosexual marriage and of homosexual persons who are celibate or who have been changed to a heterosexual lifestyle. Dialogue with those not sharing the view that homosexuality *per se* is sin is encouraged, as well as ministry to the larger homosexual community.

The second model for ministry assumes that homosexual behavior *per se* is not sin. This model calls for a general repentance and sanctification, but not necessarily repentance from homosexuality *as such*. The church should provide a nonjudgmental counseling ministry for homosexual persons and emphasize the sanctification of the homosexual estate. To aid this, the sacraments will be offered to all and the church will foster positive sex-education. Both heterosexual and homosexual persons will be held up as role models when they manifest the fruit of the Spirit. Wider dialogue with those disagreeing that homosexual behavior *per se* is not sin is also called for as well as a wider ministry to the homosexual community.

A further call is issued for full civil rights for all homosexual persons and the decriminalization of sexual acts between consenting adults.

In Part IV of the Background Paper the specific issue of ordination for avowed and practicing homosexual persons is taken up.

Those ordained to an office in the church must be gifted for their ministry and called by the church. The primary gift is the ability to proclaim God's grace to all through Jesus Christ. Secondary to this is the living of a holy life.

Within the Constitution of the United Presbyterian

Church, the Background Paper asserts that *no phrase
. . . can be construed as an explicit prohibition of the ordination of self-affirming, practicing homosexual persons
to office within the church.* This claim is made although
the Heidelberg Catechism in *the Book of Confessions* warns
that those guilty of "homosexual perversion" will not inherit the kingdom of God, and although Leviticus and Paul
designate homosexual acts as sin. These facts, it is
claimed, do not serve as a *legal* restriction to ordination.
While this *may* be true, we may also well ask whether
they do not serve as a *moral* restriction to ordination.
Furthermore, is not this moral restriction based on the
theological foundation that God created us as male and
female "from the beginning"?

In resolving the issue of the ordination of avowed and
practicing homosexual persons, the General Assembly of
the United Presbyterian Church may initiate an amend-
ment to the constitution prohibiting or affirming such ordination, or it may interpret the Constitution to bar the
ordination of avowed and practicing homosexual persons,
or it may interpret the Constitution as not barring such
ordination, or, and this is the position of the majority of
the task force, it may affirm that there is no Constitutional prohibition against ordination and choose "not to
offer an authoritative and limiting interpretation of what
may be correctly deduced from the Constitution and instead . . . (remit) the question to the presbyteries and congregations for further discussion and for adjudications
made by individual Christian consciences considering individual cases and circumstances."

While this conclusion may seem moderate, it is a dra-
matic reversal of the theological, Biblical and ethical position of the church universal for nineteen hundred years.
If the General Assembly does not close the door to the
ordination of avowed and practicing homosexual persons,

then it opens that door. If the General Assembly refuses to make a decision on ordination, it thereby makes a decision. Its decision, Scripture to the contrary, is that now avowed and practicing homosexual persons may be ordained into the United Presbyterian Church. It's saying that "gay is good."

This decision is supported because of the pluralism in the United Presbyterian Church. At issue, however, are the limits of pluralism. When does pluralism become chaos? When does pluralism become the destruction of the church? We are now at that point. Here is a great divide. If pluralism means not merely the abandoning of the Biblical teaching on homosexuality, but its denial, then pluralism has destroyed the Biblical basis for the church's identity and the authority for her Gospel and her life. Such pluralism cannot but lead to anarchy.

This decision is also supported because of "a genuine ambiguity in Biblical interpretation and of data from theology, psychotherapy, and the empirical sciences." Even the Background Paper, however, has not supported this "ambiguity" at a crucial point: the Bible teaches that homosexual acts are sinful. What then shall our standard be? Is it not perilous to decide for a new position on avowed and practicing homosexual persons on the basis of ambiguity? Is it not also perilous when the Bible is clear?

The results of a "scientific" evaluation of research data on homosexuality and a "scientific" exegesis of the Bible tend toward relativism. With no outside or foundational norms we are simply left with variable possibilities. The new standard becomes psychological and spiritual health rather than the will of God. Since "scientific" study begins with man rather than God, it should be no surprise that the outcome is an idealized homosexual person evidencing "maturing faith and self-giving love," rather than the order of God, the will of God, and the truth of God embodied in the church and the world.

Such a "scientific" evaluation, however, is not objective. It bears its own presuppositions about reason, progress, and "objectivity." The "myth of modernity" assumes that we have progressed beyond the Bible in our understanding of homosexuality. It also assumes that by the light of reason we can now fully understand God's view of homosexuality.

The "scientific evaluation," however, is employed to make a biased case. Man created as male and female is overlooked as the Biblical presupposition for understanding homosexuality. That most homosexual persons cannot be changed is assumed rather than proven. Nature rather than revelation has the final word. The ground is now laid for the destruction of the church. Losing her Biblical identity she will only wander with a lost world, adrift in a sea of relativity. To this God says, "No." To this we must say, "No," and hear again Christ's call to the Gospel and the Word of God, the unchanging rock upon which we stand.

Notes

II. Orientation and Background

1. John Rickman & Charles Brenner (eds.), *A General Selection from the Works of Sigmund Freud* (N.Y., Doubleday Anchor Books, 1957), p. 220.
2. *Ibid.*
3. *Ibid.*, pp. 220-221.
4. *Ibid.*, p. 221.
5. Cited by Lawrence Hatterer, *Changing Homosexuality in the Male* (N.Y., McGraw-Hill, 1970), p. 4.
6. *Ibid.*, p. 45.
7. *Ibid.*, p. 5.
8. Laud Humphreys, *Out of the Closets* (Englewood Cliffs, N.J., Prentice Hall, 1972), p. 60.
9. *Ibid.*
10. *Ibid.*
11. Edmund Bergler, *Homosexuality: Disease or Way of Life?* (N.Y., Collier Books, 1962), pp. 61-63.
12. C. A. Tripp, *The Homosexual Matrix* (N.Y., Signet Books, 1976) p. 220.
13. Humphreys, *op. cit.*, p. 48.
14. *Ibid.*, p. 77.
15. *Ibid.*, p. 6.
16. *Ibid.*, p. 10.
17. *Ibid.*, p. 11.
18. *Ibid.*, p. 113.
19. *Ibid.*, pp. 135-136.
20. *Ibid.*, p. 161.
21. Don Clark, *Loving Someone Gay* (Millbrae, CA, Celestial Arts, 1977) p. 106.
22. *Ibid.*, p. 107.
23. Tripp, *op. cit.*, p. 50.
24. *Ibid.*, p. 72.
25. *Ibid.*, p. 74.
26. *Ibid.*, p. 236.
27. George Weinberg, *Society and the Healthy Homosexual* (Garden City, N.Y., Anchor Books, 1973), p. xi.

28. *Ibid.*, p. 43.
29. *Ibid.*, p. 65.
30. Martin Weinberg & Colin Williams, *Male Homosexuals* (N.Y., Penguin Books, 1975), p. 18.
31. *Ibid.*, pp. 18-19.
32. *Ibid.*, p. 21.
33. *Ibid.*
34. *Ibid.*, p. 22.
35. See Clark, *op. cit.*, p. 15.
36. *Ibid.*, p. 16.

III. Contemporary Views of Homosexuality

1. Hatterer, *op. cit.*, p. 4.
2. *Ibid.*, p. 8.
3. *Ibid.*, p. 10.
4. *Ibid.*, p. 15.
5. *Ibid.*, p. 17.
6. *Ibid.*
7. *Ibid.*, p. 18.
8. *Ibid.*, p. 1.
9. *Ibid.*, p. vii.
10. *Ibid.*, p. ix Contrast the anti-homosexual therapy of Edmund Bergler, *op. cit.*.
11. *Ibid.*, p. 34.
12. *Ibid.*
13. *Ibid.*, pp. 34-35.
14. *Ibid.*, p. 35
15. *Ibid.*, p. 37.
16. *Ibid.*, p. 38.
17. *Ibid.*, p. 39.
18. *Ibid.*, pp. 39-40.
19. *Ibid.*, p. 40.
20. *Ibid.*, p. 42.
21. *Ibid.*
22. *Ibid.*, p. 43.
23. *Ibid.*, p. 47.
24. *Ibid.*, p. 44.
25. *Ibid.*, p. 57.
26. *Ibid.*, p. 60.
27. *Ibid.*, p. 59.
28. *Ibid.*, pp. 86-91.
29. *Ibid.*, p. viii.
30. *Ibid.*, p. 377.
31. Tripp, *op. cit.*, p. 8.
32. *Ibid.*
33. *Ibid.*, p. 4.
34. *Ibid.*, pp. 70-71.

35. *Ibid.*, p. 151.
36. *Ibid.*, p. 19.
37. *Ibid.*, p. 11
38. *Ibid.*, p. 14.
39. *Ibid.*, p. 11.
40. *Ibid.*, p. 14.
41. *Ibid.*, p. 11.
42. *Ibid.*, p. 33.
43. *Ibid.*, p. 36.
44. *Ibid.*, p. 43.
45. *Ibid.*, p. 55.
46. *Ibid.*, pp. 58-59.
47. *Ibid.*, p. 63.
48. *Ibid.*
49. *Ibid.*, p. 68.
50. *Ibid.*, p. 69.
51. *Ibid.*
52. *Ibid.*, pp. 75-76.
53. *Ibid.*, pp. 76-77.
54. *Ibid.*, p. 78.
55. *Ibid.*, pp. 82-83.
56. *Ibid.*, p. 84.
57. *Ibid.*, pp. 85-86.
58. *Ibid.*, p. 93.
59. *Ibid.*, p. 143.
60. *Ibid.*
61. *Ibid.*
62. *Ibid.*, p. 144.
63. *Ibid.*
64. *Ibid.*, p. 145.
65. *Ibid.*, p. 146.
66. *Ibid.*, p. 149.
67. *Ibid.*
68. *Ibid.*, p. 150.
69. *Ibid.*, p. 154.
70. *Ibid.*, p. 157.
71. *Ibid.*, p. 229.
72. *Ibid.*, p. 232.
73. *Ibid.*
74. *Ibid.*
75. *Ibid.*, p. 238.
76. *Ibid.*, p. 242.
77. *Ibid.*, pp. 244ff.
78. *Ibid.*, p. 264.
79. George Weinberg, *op. cit.*, p. xi.
80. *Ibid.*, p. 18.
81. *Ibid.*, p. 93.
82. *Ibid.*, pp. 8-17.
83. *Ibid.*, p. 20.

84. *Ibid.*, p. 30.
85. *Ibid.*, p. 61.
86. *Ibid.*, p. 64.
87. *Ibid.*, p. 69.
88. *Ibid.*, p. 72.
89. *Ibid.*, pp. 75-76.
90. *Ibid.*, p. 78.
91. *Ibid.*, p. 82.
92. *Ibid.*, p. 84.
93. *Ibid.*, pp. 84-85.
94. *Ibid.*, p. 85.
95. *Ibid.*, p. 87.
96. *Ibid.*, p. 138.
97. *Ibid.*, p. 139.
98. Clark, *op. cit.*, p. 177.
99. *Ibid.*, p. 2.
100. *Ibid.*, p. 73.
101. *Ibid.*, p. 43.
102. *Ibid.*, p. 3.
103. *Ibid.*
104. *Ibid.*, p. 5.
105. *Ibid.*, p. 51.
106. *Ibid.*
107. *Ibid.*
108. *Ibid.*, p. 38.
109. *Ibid.*, p. 9.
110. *Ibid.*, p. 22.
111. *Ibid.*, p. 122.
112. *Ibid.*, p. 32.
113. *Ibid.*, p. 12.
114. *Ibid.*, p. 22.
115. *Ibid.*, p. 118.
116. *Ibid.*, p. 184.
117. *Ibid.*, p. 29.
118. *Ibid.*, p. 30.
119. *Ibid.*, p. 33.
120. *Ibid.*, p. 34.
121. *Ibid.*, pp. 36-37.
122. *Ibid.*, p. 38.
123. *Ibid.*, p. 84.
124. *Ibid.*, p. 86.
125. *Ibid.*, p. 94.
126. *Ibid.*, p. 98.
127. *Ibid.*, p. 100.
128. *Ibid.*, p. 131.
129. *Ibid.*, p. 104.
130. *Ibid.*, p. 106.
131. *Ibid.*, p. 3.

IV. The Biblical Teaching

1. D. S. Bailey, *Homosexuality and the Western Christian Tradition* (London: Longmans, Green & Co., 1955); R. Treese in S. Gearhart and W. R. Johnson, *Loving Women, Loving Men* (San Francisco: Glide, 1974); J. McNeill, *The Church and the Homosexual* (Kansas City: Sheed Andrews & McMeill, 1976).

2. Von Rad holds that the majority of the early narratives in Genesis were aetiologies, *Genesis* (Philadelphia: Westminster, 1961), p. 17.

3. *Ibid.*, p. 23.

4. *Ibid.*

5. *Ibid.*, p. 26.

6. *Ibid.*, p. 31.

7. Paul Jewett, *Man as Male and Female* (Grand Rapids: Eerdmans, 1975), p. 122 n. 95.

8. see Von Rad, *op. cit.*, p. 41.

9. As Von Rad notes, "Genesis, Ch. 1., begins the *work of history*, which continues to the revelation at Sinai and the tribal conquest." *Ibid.*, p. 63.

10. *Ibid.*, p. 47 and Walther Eichrodt, *Theology of the Old Testament*, Vol. I (Philadelphia: Westminster, 1967), p. 103.

11. Eichrodt, *op. cit.*, p. 99.

12. *Ibid.*, p. 101.

13. Von Rad, *op. cit.*, pp. 49-50.

14. *Ibid.*, p. 49.

15. See Eichrodt, *op. cit.*, p. 109.

16. *Ibid.*, pp. 124-125.

17. Noted in Jewett, *op. cit.*, p. 35 n. 17.

18. cf. G. Kittel, *Theological Dictionary of the New Testament*, Vol. II (Grand Rapids: Eerdmans, 1964), pp. 390ff.

19. Von Rad, *op. cit.*, p. 56; Eichrodt, *op. cit.*, p. 122.

20. Von Rad, *op. cit.*, p. 56.

21. *Ibid.*

22. Eichrodt, *op. cit.*, p. 123.

23. Von Rad, *op. cit.*, p. 56.

24. Eichrodt, *op. cit.*, p. 126. See also Jewett, *op cit.*, p. 21.

25. Von Rad, *op. cit.*, p. 58.

26. Jewett, *op. cit.*, p. 36.

27. As Von Rad notes, "The idea of man . . . finds its full meaning not in the male alone but in man and woman." *Op. cit.*, p. 58.

28. Jewett, *op. cit.*, p. 24.

29. McNeill, *op. cit.*, p. 60.

30. Von Rad, *op. cit.*, p. 58.

31. *Ibid.*, p. 59.

32. See Eichrodt, *op. cit.*, p. 128.

33. *Ibid.*, p. 108.

34. Von Rad, *op. cit.*, p. 59.

35. *Ibid.*, p. 24.

36. *Ibid.*, p. 75.

37. *Ibid.*, p. 74.

38. *Ibid.*, p. 80.

39. Eichrodt, *op. cit.*, p. 121.
40. Karl Barth *Church Dogmatics*, III/1 (Edinburgh: T&T Clark, 1958) p. 331.
41. Von Rad, *op. cit.*, p. 82.
42. *Ibid.*, p. 79.
43. See Karl Barth, *The Epistle to the Romans* (N.Y.: Oxford, 1972).
44. Von Rad, *op. cit.*, p. 206.
45. *Ibid.*, p. 208.
46. *Ibid.*, p. 209.
47. *Ibid.*, p. 214.
48. Bailey, *op. cit.*, p. 4.
49. *Ibid.*, p. 3.
50. *Ibid.*, pp. 9-10.
51. *Ibid.*, p. 10.
52. McNeill, *op. cit.*, p. 47.
53. Von Rad, *op. cit.*, p. 216.
54. *Ibid.*, pp. 212-213.
55. McNeill, *op. cit.*, p. 48.
56. Treese in Gearhart and Johnson, *op. cit.*, p. 33.
57. Bailey, *op. cit.*, p. 37. Also Von Rad, *op. cit.*, p. 212.
58. Eichrodt, *Theology of the Old Testament*, Vol. I, p. 75.
59. *Ibid.*, pp. 75-80.
60. *Ibid.*, p. 80.
61. *Ibid.*, p. 82.
62. *Ibid.*, p. 425.
63. *Ibid.*, p. 404.
64. D. S. Bailey, *op. cit.*, p. 29.
65. Martin Noth, *Leviticus* (Philadelphia: Westminster, 1965), p. 16.
66. *Ibid.*, p. 136.
67. It is apodictic in style, *Ibid.*, p. 134.
68. N. H. Snaith, *Leviticus and Numbers* (London: Nelson, 1967), p. 125.
69. *Ibid.*
70. *Ibid.*, p. 126.
71. Noth, *op. cit.*, p. 136.
72. Bailey, *op. cit.*, p. 53.
73. *Ibid.*, p. 36.
74. *Ibid.*, p. 30.
75. Noth, *op. cit.*, p. 146.
76. *Ibid.*
77. *Ibid.*, p. 147.
78. McNeill, *op. cit.*, p. 58.
79. *Ibid.*, p. 57.
80. Bailey, *op. cit.*, p. 60.
81. Similarly in Leviticus 18:23 a woman lying with a beast is a "perversion," or literally a "confusion." Snaith admits this could mean a violation of nature and, based on Genesis 1, it certainly does, *op. cit.*, p. 126.
82. Von Rad, *op. cit.*, p. 213.
83. John Gray, *Joshua, Judges and Ruth* (London: Nelson, 1967), p. 372.

84. Robert Boling, *Judges* (Garden City, N.Y.: Doubleday, 1975), p. 279.
85. Bailey, *op. cit.*, p. 54.
86. *Ibid.*, p. 279.
87. Gray, *op. cit.*, p. 378.
88. Denied by Bailey who uses the same arguments as in Genesis 19, *op. cit.*, p. 54.
89. So too Paul in I Corinthians 7.
90. Bailey, *op. cit.*, p. 23.
91. *Ibid.*, p. 27.
92. Quite certainly Paul writes from Corinth, See W. Sanday and A. C. Headlam, *The Epistle to the Romans* (N.Y.: Scribner's, 1896), pp. xxxvi ff.
93. Bailey, *op. cit.*, p. 40.
94. *Ibid.*, p. 41. See also Treese, in Gearhart and Johnson, *op. cit.*, pp. 36-37.
95. See McNeill, *op. cit.*, p. 53.
96. *Ibid.*, p. 54.
97. *Ibid.*, p. 56.
98. *Ibid.*
99. See Koster, *Phusis* in G. Friedrich (ed.), *Theological Dictionary of the New Testament*, Vol. IX (Grand Rapids: Eerdmans, 1974), p. 271.
100. C. K. Barrett, *A Commentary on the Epistle to the Romans* (N.Y.: Harper & Row, 1957), p. 39.
101. In an unpublished paper, George Edwards, "Romans 1:26-27 and Homosexuality: A study in Context," 1975.
102. See W. D. Davies, *Paul and Rabbinic Judaism* (London: S.P.C.K., 1947).
103. Bailey, *op. cit.*, p. xi.
104. *Ibid.*
105. Tresse, in Gearhart and Johnson, *op. cit.*, p. 38.
106. McNeill, *op. cit.*, p. 42.
107. *Ibid.*, p. 55.
108. Hans Conzelmann, *I Corinthians* (Philadelphia: Fortress, 1975), p. 106.
109. C. K. Barrett, *A Commentary on the First Epistle to the Corinthians* (N.Y.: Harper & Row, 1968), p. 140.
110. Conzelmann, *op. cit.*, p. 106.
111. *Ibid.*
112. Barrett, *I Corinthians*, p. 140.
113. W. Bauer, *A Greek-English Lexicon of the New Testament* (Chicago: University of Chicago Press, 1957), p. 489.
114. *Ibid.*, p. 109.
115. McNeill, *op. cit.*, p. 52.
116. *Ibid.*
117. *Ibid.*
118. *Ibid.*, p. 53.
119. *Ibid.*
120. Bauer, *op. cit.*, p. 700.
121. Bailey, *op. cit.*, p. 38 n. 2.

122. See *A Lexicon Abridged From Liddell and Scott's Greek-English Lexicon* (Oxford: Clarendon Press, 1953), p. 104. The word compounds ARSEV & KOITE.

123. Bailey, *op. cit.*, p. 38.

124. Tresse in Gearhart and Johnson, *op. cit.*, p. 39.

125. See J. N. D. Kelley, *A Commentary on the Pastoral Epistles* (N.Y.: Harper, 1963), p. 34.

126. See M. Dibelius and H. Conzelmann, *The Pastoral Epistles* (Philadelphia, Fortress, 1972), pp. 1ff.

127. *Ibid.*, p. 23.

128. *Ibid.*

129. *Ibid.*

130. Kelly, *op. cit.*, p. 50.

131. For a detailed exposition of this see Don Williams, *The Apostle Paul and Women in the Church* (Van Nuys, CA. BIM, 1977).

132. G. H. Boobyer, "Jude" in M. Black, *Peake's Commentary on the Bible* (London: Nelson, 1962), p. 1041.

133. C. Bigg, *The Epistles of St. Peter and St. Jude* (Edinburgh: T&T Clark, 1902), p. 318.

134. *Ibid.*, p. 321.

135. Boobyer in Black, *op. cit.*, p. 1041.

136. T. Leahy, "The Epistle of Jude" in Brown, Fitzmyer & Murphy (eds.), *The Jerome Biblical Commentary* (Englewood Cliffs, N.Y.: Prentice-Hall, 1968), p. 379.

137. William H. Brownlee, "The Meaning of Fornication," an unpublished paper read to San Gabriel Presbytery, CA, Nov. 19. 1977.

138. McNeill, *op. cit.*, pp. 70-71.

139. Bailey, *op. cit.*, pp. 11ff.

140. *Ibid.*, p. 16.

V. The Theologians

1. Bailey, *op. cit.*, p. viii.

2. See Karl Barth, *op. cit.*, III. 1.

3. Barth, *Church Dogmatics* (Edinburgh: T&T Clark, 1961), III. 4.

4. *Ibid.*, p. 166.

5. Barth, *Church Dogmatics*, III. 1., p. 3.

6. *Ibid.*, p. 24.

7. *Ibid.*, pp. 25-26.

8. *Ibid.*, p. 42.

9. *Ibid.*, p. 43.

10. *Ibid.*, p. 59.

11. *Ibid.*, p. 97.

12. *Ibid.*, p. 61.

13. *Ibid.*, p. 62.

14. *Ibid.*, p. 67.

15. *Ibid.*, p. 80.

16. *Ibid.*, p. 98.

17. *Ibid.*, p. 184.
18. *Ibid.*, p. 192. This finds its ultimate expression in the doctrine of the Trinity.
19. *Ibid.*, p. 185.
20. Barth, *Church Dogmatics* (Edinburgh: T&T Clark, 1960), III. 2., p. 285.
21. *Ibid.*, p. 286.
22. *Ibid.*, p. 289.
23. Barth, *Church Dogmatics* III. 1., p. 186.
24. *Ibid.*, pp. 186-187.
25. *Ibid.*, p. 189.
26. Barth, *Church Dogmatics*, III. 4., p. 132.
27. *Ibid.*, p. 133.
28. *Ibid.*, p. 154.
29. Barth, *Church Dogmatics*, III. 1., p. 291.
30. *Ibid.*, p. 294.
31. *Ibid.*, p. 299.
32. *Ibid.*, p. 300.
33. *Ibid.*, p. 190.
34. *Ibid.*, p. 310.
35. *Ibid.*, p. 290.
36. Barth, *Church Dogmatics*, III. 4., p. 156.
37. *Ibid.*, pp. 156ff.
38. *Ibid.*, p. 159.
39. *Ibid.*, p. 158.
40. *Ibid.*, p. 166
41. *Ibid.*
42. *Ibid.*
43. *Ibid.*
44. *Ibid.*
45. H. Thielicke, *The Ethics of Sex* (N.Y.: Harper & Row, 1964), p. 3.
46. *Ibid.*, p. 4.
47. *Ibid.*, p. 5.
48. *Ibid.*, p. 4.
49. *Ibid.*, p. 3.
50. *Ibid.*, p. 13.
51. *Ibid.*, p. 3.
52. *Ibid.*, p. 5.
53. *Ibid.*, p. 6.
54. *Ibid.*, pp. 6ff.
55. *Ibid.*, p. 3 n. 2.
56. *Ibid.*, p. 282.
57. *Ibid.*, p. 283.
58. *Ibid.*
59. *Ibid.*
60. *Ibid.*
61. *Ibid.*, p. 282.

62. *Ibid.*, p. 277.
63. *Ibid.*, p. 278.
64. *Ibid.*, p. 281.
65. *Ibid.*, p. 283.
66. *Ibid.*
67. *Ibid.*, p. 284.
68. *Ibid.*
69. *Ibid.*, p. 285.
70. *Ibid.*, pp. 284ff.
71. *Ibid.*, p. 285.
72. *Ibid.*
73. *Ibid.*, p. 271.
74. *Ibid.*
75. McNeill, *op. cit.*, p. 65.
76. *Ibid.*, pp. 89ff.
77. *Ibid.*, p. 15.
78. *Ibid.*, p. 105.
79. *Ibid.*, p. 106.
80. *Ibid.*, p. 4.
81. *Ibid.*, pp. 18-19.
82. *Ibid.*, p. 110.
83. *Ibid.*, p. 38.
84. *Ibid.*, p. 49.
85. *Ibid.*, pp. 57-58.
86. *Ibid.*, p. 39.
87. *Ibid.*, p. 56.
88. *Ibid.*, pp. 39.
89. *Ibid.*, p. 66.
90. *Ibid.*, p. 100.
91. *Ibid.*, p. 101.
92. *Ibid.*, pp. 102-103.
93. *Ibid.*, p. 132.
94. *Ibid.*, p. 133.
95. *Ibid.*, p. 134.
96. *Ibid.*, p. 132.
97. *Ibid.*, pp. 138ff.
98. *Ibid.*, pp. 141ff.
99. *Ibid.*, p. 145.
100. *Ibid.*, p. 145.
101. *Ibid.*, p. 140.
102. *Ibid.*, p. 147.
103. *Ibid.*
104. *Ibid.*, p. 161. Where then go all of McNeill's ideals about homosexual "wholeness"?
105. From Richard F. Hettlinger, *Living with Sex: The Student's Dilemma*, pp. 94-112, cited by McNeill, p. 162.
106. *Ibid.*, p. 178.

VI. Conclusion

1. John Money and Patricia Tucker, *Sexual Signatures* (Boston: Little, Brown, & Co., 1975), p. 5.

2. *Ibid.*, pp. 87-88. The gender identity locks by about 18 months after birth.

3. See, *Ibid.*, p. 16 and pp. 25-30.